CARMELITE MONASTERY
VERMONT

W9-ADD-713

PARABLES AND INSTRUCTIONS IN THE GOSPELS

Parables and Instructions in the Gospels

HEINRICH KAHLEFELD

Translated by
Arlene Swidler

HERDER AND HERDER

226.80b
Kap

1966
HERDER AND HERDER NEW YORK
232 Madison Avenue, New York 10016

Original edition:
Gleichnisse und Lehrstücke im Evangelium,
Josef Knecht, Frankfurt am Main, 1963.

Nihil obstat: Thomas J. Beary
Censor Librorum
Imprimatur: Patrick C. Brennan
Vicar General, Diocese of Burlington
November 1, 1965
The *Nihil obstat* and *Imprimatur* are official declarations that a book or pamphlet is considered to be free of doctrinal and moral error. No implication is contained therein that those who have granted the *Nihil obstat* and *Imprimatur* agree with the contents, opinions, or statements expressed.

226.87
K p

Library of Congress Catalog Card Number: 66–13073
© 1966 by Herder and Herder, Incorporated
Manufactured in the United States of America

Contents

Foreword, by Raymond E. Brown, S.S.   7

Introduction   11

I. THE GOSPEL AND ITS POWER   15

The sowing (Mk. 4, 3–9) *15*. The growing seed (Mk.
4, 26–29) *23*. The mustard seed (Mk. 4, 30–32) *24*.
The leaven (Lk. 13, 20f.; Mt. 13, 33) *26*. The explanation of the parable of the sowing (Mk. 4, 14–20) *27*.
The meaning of speaking in parables (Mk. 4, 33–34)
33. Summary *37*.

II. THE MESSIANIC ERA   40

Introduction *40*. The fig tree (Mk. 13, 28f.) *42*. The
wedding (Mk. 2, 18–22) *45*. The weeds in the field
(Mt. 13, 24–30) *51*. The catching of fish (Mt. 13, 47–
50) *58*. The explanation of the parable of the weeds
(Mt. 13, 36–43) *60*.

III. THE WARNING TO ISRAEL   67

Introduction *67*. The unfruitful fig tree (Lk. 13, 6–9)
68. The peevish children (Lk. 7, 31–34) *70*. The rebellious vine-dressers (Mk. 12, 1–9; Mt. 21, 33–41; Lk.
20, 9–16) *72*. The great banquet (Mt. 22, 2–10; Lk. 14,
16–24) *80*. The wedding garment (Mt. 22, 11–14) *84*.

IV. PREPAREDNESS   103

Introduction *103*. The watchful householder (Lk. 12, 39f.) *105*. The doorkeeper (Mk. 13, 34–37) *106*. The faithful and the wicked servants (Mt. 24, 45–51; Lk. 12, 41–46) *108*. The waiting servants (Lk. 12, 35–38) *112*. The ten maidens (Mt. 25, 1–13) *117*.

V. THE CONTRIBUTION   125

Introduction *125*. Building a tower and waging a war (Lk. 14, 28–32) *126*. The buried talent (Mt. 25, 14–30; Lk. 19, 12–27) *132*. The treasure and the pearl (Mt. 13, 44–46) *150*.

Notes   156

Biblical References   169

Foreword

The parables constitute one of the aspects of the Gospels most affected by the modern developments in exegesis. Because so much of Jesus' message and teaching was enshrined in the parables, these stories became the subject of intensive catechesis and explanation from the earliest days of Christianity. Only now are we beginning to realize that by the time the synoptic Gospels were written the parables of Jesus had already undergone considerable development. The lessons that they taught had already been adapted to new situations in Church life; their settings and audiences had been changed; details had been altered in the process of oral transmission; once separate parables had been grouped and even welded together; sayings had been joined to them which put a new emphasis on the original parable. Thus, we often have the phenomenon that the same parable may be interpreted in different ways in different Gospels.

Nor did the development of parable exegesis stop with the New Testament. The patristic period brought to the fore an approach to the parables that was only incipient in the written Gospels, namely, the allegorization of the parables. As told by Jesus, the parables were simple stories with one principal point (and, at times, a subordinate point). The details were significant only in as much as they contributed to making the one point. But as the parables were retold in the later Church, there was a systematic attempt to see meaning in each detail of the parable as if one were dealing with an elaborate allegory. In the parable of the

7

Good Samaritan, for example, the interpreter searched for significance in the fact that the man's wounds were treated with *oil and wine* and that his bruised body was placed on a *donkey*—a hidden symbolism was seen in such incidentals. It was legitimate to ask who was being represented by the innkeeper who took care of the man. Influential ecclesiastical writers like Sts. Augustine and Gregory the Great composed intricate allegorical explanations of the parables, using Jesus' stories as a catechetical textbook for teaching the whole of Christian doctrine. Laudable as this purpose may have been, the interpretation was often quite far removed from the original import of Jesus' own presentation. Nevertheless, this patristic allegorical exegesis passed into the liturgical readings of the Church and served as the guideline for the approach of the scholastic theologians to the parables. Indeed, it dominated the interpretation of the parables right up to our own century.

The reaction came from liberal Protestant exegesis, personified in Adolf Jülicher who in 1888–89 wrote two volumes on the parables, vigorously rejecting allegorization. He went too far in this rejection, for in his absolute distinction between parable and allegory he failed to recognize that there were some elements of simple allegory even in Jesus' unsophisticated preaching. He did clear the way, however, for a fresh approach to the parables. Jülicher was a victim of his own liberal outlook; he thought of Jesus somewhat in the manner of a nineteenth-century moralist—a gentle teacher of universal ethics. Therefore, Jülicher failed in his attempt to reconstruct the original context in which the parables were uttered. Such a reconstruction became more of a possibility when liberalism lost its appeal in exegesis, and Jesus was restored to the first-century Jewish world with its atmosphere of violent apocalyptic expectations, binding Mosaic Law, and bitter conflicts among Jewish sects. A series of impressive Protestant works on the parables (A. T. Cadoux, C. H. Dodd, B. T. D. Smith, C. W. F. Smith, J. Jeremias, and W. Michaelis) carried on and modified the approach initiated by Jülicher. There emerged a critical exegesis which could distinguish with some assurance between the original import of the stories of Jesus and the development that these stories had undergone in the Gospel tradition. Although some of these exegetes unfortunately tended to depreciate the importance and value of the interpretative insights of the evangelists, they did revive for the Christian world the fresh impact of the parable as it was uttered by Jesus during his ministry.

In this modern development of parable exegesis the contribution of Catholic scholarship has been relatively modest. Too many of the numerous Catholic books on the subject simply combed the Fathers for allegorical material and contented themselves with explaining some of the obscure details of the stories. The most serious study in the early part of the century was that of the Jesuit exegete Leopold Fonck, a study translated into many languages. Despite its erudition, Fonck's treatment failed completely in the critical task of distinguishing between Jesus and the evangelists—a task now insisted upon both by the Pontifical Biblical Commission and by Vatican II in its decree on revelation. In a French work of the 1930s Denis Buzy showed a much better critical sense; moreover, his firsthand knowledge of Palestine supplied some very useful information for understanding rural customs alluded to in the parables. Another Catholic scholar, M. Hermaniuk, subjected Jülicher's overexact distinction between parable and allegory to a much needed modification. Yet one must admit that in general we were far behind our Protestant brethren in the real exegesis of the parables. Since the War, Catholics have been producing excellent studies on points of parable

9

exegesis and on individual parables (L. Cerfaux, M. De Goedt, J. Dupont, A. George, M. Didier, E. Siegman are some of the names that come immediately to mind). Yet there has been no complete modern treatment of the parables by a Catholic—a treatment that would give both Catholic theologians and parish priests a thorough treatment of each parable and a firm guide in approaching parable exegesis.

I shall not claim that this short work by Father Kahlefeld is the complete work of which I have spoken. But it is an important step towards what we need and will help many in understanding the modern approach to the parables. Those accustomed to an older parable exegesis will find themselves in a new world here. Unfortunately, this may cause difficulty, for some will find it annoying that the parables are interpreted in a different way from that which they thought traditional. Others will resent the fact that the parables have to be studied so carefully with painstaking use of critical exegetical tools. Father Kahlefeld's book is a solid piece of scholarship that can help the attentive reader in the task of studying the parables. In a number of points I would disagree with his exegesis; yet his views are always worthy of scholarly respect. In fact, the very existence of such occasional disagreement between two Catholic exegetes is a testimony to a maturer attitude in Catholic biblical studies. The thought that there must be a uniform Catholic exegesis is an oversimplification based on the failure to understand that interpreting Scripture is a human endeavor. The Church can speak definitively on the meaning of a passage but seldom does so, leaving her children to use their own intelligence under her general guidance.

RAYMOND E. BROWN, S.S.
St. Mary's Seminary
Roland Park, Baltimore

Introduction

The title of this book places alongside the parable a closely connected but differently constructed literary form, the instruction. When it is told of a salesman that upon his return home at night he found the gatekeeper awake and praised him for it, and from this story follows an exhortation to prepare for another, a greater event, then a transfer occurs: What is to be understood in the tale and in the passage emphasized by the explanation is actually valid on the higher plane. Thus we have a parable.

But when it is told of a salesman that while on a journey he helped an unfortunate man and took his problems upon himself and did everything to rescue him, then there is nothing to transfer; instead, the hearer is told: "Do likewise!" Such a story is meaningful in its every feature; whether it brings before our eyes a picture of good and wise conduct, as in the case of the salesman, or of foolish and mistaken attitudes, as in the case of the praying Pharisee, it presents it to the hearers as vividly as possible in order to say afterwards in the form of a dictum what positive or negative truth is to be learned from it. Dictum and story form a tight unity; the dictum does not contribute, as in the case of the parable, to the comprehension of the moral, which lies completely in the story itself; rather, in this case the tale helps to make the moral of the dictum clear. To be precise, we speak of this structure as an "instruction."

But the two literary forms are placed alongside one another in the title only because from the beginning it must be understood that the concept of parable is here understood more narrowly than is customary in sermons and lessons. This primary distinction is a valid one, and both these forms are actually opposed to that other different form which is not at all concerned with telling a story drawn from life and revealing a higher insight through it, but rather establishes its story on a higher plane at once and expresses a recognizable issue or connection through earthly figures of speech and incidents. It "says something else" than what it seems to say, and is therefore called an "allegory."

This difference is much more important than the first; indeed, for exegesis it is the only one of importance. Whether there is pure allegory in the material of the synoptic tradition is a moot question. But there is no question but that rudimentary parable structures permeated with allegorical features or accompanied by allegorizing additions can be found. Whether we are dealing here with originally "mixed forms," or whether the attempt to grasp and detach one layer from secondary interpretations in order to get the original parable into focus is worthwhile, —this is all yet to be tested. A person who takes pleasure in allegorical speech will find such work idle and perhaps disturbing. He will probably be inclined to push the allegorizing farther for his part, and to complete it and think to himself that only now is the whole truth of the mysterious passage given its due and its real sense learned.

But the man who can think only in historical terms and recognize the hand of God in the historical events of revelation will accordingly insist upon understanding Jesus' original words as clearly as possible. And, at the same time, he will not be amazed that a living tradition, motivated by faith, has been deposited upon the form of the original language, and has occasionally penetrated through into it. He will realize that the early preach-

12

ing which is perceived there must be respected, and he will understand that the proclamation does not wish to exist alongside the words of the Lord but to be most closely united with them.

The exegesis presented here is determined by such insights. It accepts the historical view of the material which the canonical Gospels offer as the good and right way to theological perception and at the same time to spiritual insight.

It is obvious, then, that some effort will be demanded of the reader; but that is not all. He is expressly asked for patience and understanding and a prepayment of confidence, so that he will not have misgivings about the kind of investigation that is undertaken here. The justification of the method will be accomplished through its result. And so there is one further request: the reader must be willing to give the book a real reading straight through from the beginning to the end.

Because exegesis asks questions about the contents of the parables, an attempt has been made to put the material in a thematic order. But this is permissible only when we add that in more than one case the grouping could well have been made quite differently, and that the heading given is not intended to constitute a "generic term." The reader should be able to linger a while with one theme and to see how one parable assists another.

Because the material in being worked over repeatedly has grown beyond the anticipated limits, and yet the book is intended to accompany the reader "in his pocket," only one part is taken up here. A second volume will take up the following: the mind of God, the attitude towards God, conduct towards one's neighbor. At the end there will be a few summarizing statements to be made about the uniqueness of the parable, with which research since the 'thirties is again so urgently occupied. The second volume will also contain a subject index to the two volumes, an index of technical terms, and a bibliography listing the more significant works in the last decades on exegesis of the parables.

I.

The Gospel and Its Power

The section of Mark's Gospel which constitutes the fourth chapter seems at first glance to be a straightforward report of an incident, moving on through several scenes, yet unified. But on closer inspection a complicated arrangement of older and newer traditional materials reveals itself. An early, still very simple, compilation of sayings of the Lord appears to have been materially expanded in the process of being handed on and to have been provided with new emphases, so that there has arisen a complex, powerful piece of early Christian proclamation which has played a significant role in the formation of the written Gospel.

The kernel of the composition and evidently its oldest layer is composed of three parables: that of the sowing, that of the growing seed, and that of the mustard seed.

These three will be considered now.

1.

MK. 4, 3–9:

3 "Listen! A sower went out to sow. *4*And as he sowed, some seed fell along the path, and the birds came and devoured it. *5*Other seed fell on rocky ground, where it had not much soil, and immediately it sprang up, since it had no depth of soil; *6*and when the sun rose it was scorched, and since it had no root it withered away. *7*Other seed fell among thorns and the thorns grew up and choked it, and it yielded no grain. *8*And other seeds fell into good soil and brought

15

forth grain, growing up and increasing and yielding thirtyfold and sixtyfold and a hundredfold." [9]And he said, "He who has ears to hear, let him hear."

First of all there are a few separate observations to be made:

v. 3: The summons "Listen" and the other in verse 9, "He who has ears to hear, let him hear," frame the parable. They demand that what is said there be considered carefully. But that means that they give no information about the contents of the discourse; it is not said that the parable itself should be a warning to hear rightly. There is, therefore, more to be asked about its meaning.

v. 4: It is to be noted of this work of sowing that it is a documented fact that in olden days, just as today, it was customary when planting before the rainy season to throw out the seed after a pre-ploughing and then to plough it under afterwards. The farmer carries his seed in a sack hung around him or caught up in a fold of his long garment. He throws the grain out in steady, even strokes, and when he has paced off and sown the strips, the plough follows and turns the seed under the earth. This fact throws light on the situations which are described in the parable.

Alongside the neighboring plot the field is bordered by a heavily trod path, so the sower must see that he does not lose too much on this path, for the birds are already waiting; because of them no strips are sown unless they can be ploughed in the same session.

vv. 5-6: In the hilly country the arable land is generally won from the stony soil. A part of the rock has crumbled to earth, but many fragments still are mixed with the soil, and in many places the rock lies under a thin cover of earth. This is not discernible in the sowing, but only when the plough comes. The plough must be lifted up so that it is not smashed on the rock. What is sowed in such a place can, if the birds do not take it, sprout very quickly, because the rock, heated by the sun, holds the earth warm in the night, and the morning dew penetrates quickly. But the blades are soon burnt by the sun.[1]

v. 7: The farmer must constantly battle with the rank weeds, especially with the luxuriant man-high thistles—these are probably what is meant by the "thorns." The seed must therefore be carefully sorted, and even the growing field must still be weeded.[2] Above all, the roots of the "thorns" must be hoed out; what is spared will shoot up exuberantly and overgrow everything else.

v. 8: In the hilly areas "good soil" means a piece of land that has few stones, and, in general, whatever brings a good return. In the parable it obviously means that part within the same plot which neither lies on the hard-trod path nor is hindered in its fruitfulness by rock or weeds. As far as the harvest of the field is concerned, in the hills one is content with a tenfold yield, but in the Jordan Valley and on the coast the barley can actually be fruitful even to a hundredfold. However, such a rich yield is seen as an especial sign of blessing, as the most that can be expected.[3]

Thus the tale speaks of incidents which are well known to its hearers. It is the striking description of the intimately familiar that gives the discourse its force.

* * *

If one goes on to ask about the meaning of the piece, the answer seems simple at first. In the composition the disciples do specifically ask about this meaning, and the parable is explained to them (Mk. 4, 10. 13. 14–20). But parable and interpretation are not as closely related as they may seem at first glance. The interpreta-

17

tion, of course, belongs to the traditional material which Mark had already found present, and as such it must still be treated later; however, it appears likely that the assumption to be followed even now is that the three parables originally had formed a closed unity, not interspersed with other matter. But that means that the first of these must be as understandable without such an explanation as the second and third. It is such an understanding that we must now seek.

The genuine parable rests on one tale. Its metaphorical function is customarily disclosed by an additional element which indicates the salient point, the decisive incident from which the transfer to the level of significance arises. This "key" may follow the tale, but it can also introduce it. The text of the sowing lacks such an element. The example of other parables shows that occasionally such a key was obviously not necessary because the situation in which Jesus spoke was itself able to make the meaning of the discourse clear. When the parable of the shepherd who wishes to regain his sheep is told to those who take scandal at his friendliness to sinners, the meaning is clear without a "key." And we cannot be really certain that such an aid was given for the parable of the sowing. The sketch of the situation, which preceded in the text of Mark (4, 1–2), belongs to the frame of the composition and does not contribute much to its interpretation.

The meaning of the piece, therefore, is not easy to find, and there are exegetes who despair of it.[4] Nevertheless, the approach does not seem sealed. For it must be borne in mind that those early conveyors of the tradition who joined the three parables together in a group must have known their meaning and taken for granted that the readers and hearers also could understand it. How is that possible?

18

First of all, it must be supposed that they had already connected this group of three with the first acts of Jesus in Galilee, and therefore that Mark was already following a model when he offered an example of the early proclamation along with these parables.[5] If that is true, it would be well to seek a meaning for the discourse which suits that original phase of Jesus' public life. This will be a great help.

After that we must note how the group of three parables is bound together. The first is without any "key"; the second contains a short introductory formula: "The kingdom of heaven is as if this"; the third has the full parable-introduction customary in the Jewish teaching tradition: "With what can we compare the kingdom of God, or what parable shall we use for it?" The formula is, of course, too universal to reveal the meaning of the piece, but it does nevertheless prove that any meaning suggested should be connected with the event that Jesus was announcing prophetically. Because there is also an inclination to give a key once for a series of parables, placing it at the end,[6] it may be assumed that the earlier transmitters of the tradition understood the entire group, and thus also the first parable, as a discourse on the things of the kingdom of God. But then it must also be assumed that the three pieces are linked together not only through a common catch-word, the "seed," but also through their meanings.

Thus three approaches to the exegesis suggest themselves, each of which qualifies and completes the others: 1) Each parable is to be investigated individually first of all, and to be considered in the light of its plan, its structure, the emphases within it, the application of certain images, and other matters. 2) The provisionally established meaning of the individual parable must then

19

from time to time be compared with the other two to determine where they differ from one another and where they confirm one another. 3) The individual and the common meanings must be placed within the perspective of the over-all proclamation as it is recognizable in other passages handed down by tradition. The thematic agreement or association can corroborate the exegesis.

The first parable describes the different fates of the seed, determined by the kind of earth on which they fall. Here an intensification takes place: the seed is annihilated, the young blade is annihilated, the grown plant is annihilated. After this negative progression the shift into the positive appears all the clearer: a rich success stands in contrast to all the misfortune. The story is, therefore, although it proceeds in four steps, twofold in its structure. The presentation of the misfortune, with its three steps, matches that of the success as the "indeed" matches the "however." The weight of the conclusion—again and again a confirming rhetorical moment—lies upon the success, and its description has about it the tone of a happy experience: thirty-, sixty-, even a hundredfold is the yield.

The discourse is thus an expression of confidence. But what we now have to investigate is the situation which should be considered with such confidence.

The tale is concentrated on the incident of the sowing; it tells what happened "as he sowed" (4, 4). One should stop there if he is seeking the meaning of the parable. Certainly, it is the sower who sows, but it is not he with his hopes, cares, and joys who stands as the center of attention; the story concerns only the work of sowing.[7]

On the other hand, it must be noted that the incidents of sowing already had a metaphorical meaning in the Jewish tradition, and such previous meanings play a role, as we shall see later, in the construction of the parable. Thus, when it is remembered that in late-Jewish scriptures it is said in the name of God, "Israel, hear me; today I sow my law in your heart, which should bring forth fruit in you . . . ," and it is further stated that they who possessed the law have gone astray, "because they had not preserved what was sowed in them" (4 Esdras 9, 30–33), it can be supposed that Jesus' hearers were already guided by the fact that the discourse was about sowing and its success or failure to recognize that the work of God corresponds to the revelation of the law.[8]

If one accepts tentatively that the parable has the "good news" in mind, it can be recognized how the discourse fits into the situation at the beginning of Jesus' public life. Mark begins his presentation with the words: "Jesus came into Galilee, preaching the gospel of God, and saying, 'The time is fulfilled, and the kingdom of God is at hand; repent, and believe in the gospel'" (Mk. 1, 14–15). There then follows a long series of reports, all of which conclude that the people of Galilee are overwhelmed by His powerful prophetic discourses (1, 22. 27–28. 38–40. 45; 2, 2. 13; 3, 31–35), which in turn are borne out by prophetic signs (1, 23–28. 32–34. 40–43; 2, 8–12; 3, 1–6. 7–12. 22–27). If one allows himself to be influenced by the presentation of the first three chapters, it becomes very obvious what they are trying to demonstrate: the work of Jesus was crowned by that success which can only be explained by the power of the Spirit of God. For He was anointed by God "with the Holy Spirit and with power" (Acts 10, 38; cf. Lk. 4, 18), He had received the effective power through which the Messiah fulfilled His office, and the people of Israel had acknowledged with fear and amazement that He spoke "as one

21

who had authority" (Mk. 1, 22). Then in the reports in the second chapter opposition shows itself for the first time. It comes from the authorities. The clear vision of their disciplined thinking becomes aware of a decision of enormous consequence and opposes it from the beginning (cf. 2, 7. 16. 24; 3, 2. 22). The opposition, of course, does change Jesus' working method, but it does not break the force of the prophetic proclamation. The passage on the battle with Satan in the middle of the third chapter (3, 20–30) makes this clear. This theme is held through the entire presentation up to the end of the passion.

The conviction that the effective word of God is irresistible belongs to the prophetic consciousness. Yahweh says in the Book of Jeremiah, "Is not my word fire, and like a hammer which breaks this rock in pieces?" (23, 29), and in the Book of Isaiah there appears a statement of God, "For as the rain and the snow come down from heaven, and return not thither but water the earth, making it bring forth and sprout, giving seed to the sower and bread to the eater, so shall my word be that goes forth from my mouth; it shall not return to me empty, but it shall accomplish that which I purpose, and prosper in the thing for which I sent it" (55, 10–11). Thus Jesus' confidence becomes comprehensible; but another meaning is also recognizable—He professes this confidence before His disciples and makes it understandable to them: not only should they believe what the message announces and recognize the force of the event that stands in the future, but they must also learn to trust in the moving strength that already works in His proclamation.

So the meaning of the parable and the situation in which it was originally spoken can be known with some certainty. The work of proclamation is in full progress, but the first opposition

22

and above all the law of inertia are also noticeable. To all this, faith, of which it is said that it can "move mountains" (Mt. 17, 20), answers, "Nevertheless . . ."

What the parable has to say is not bound indissolubly to the original situation. Its summons is valid for everyone who is convinced that the work of the Last Judgment will bring to completion what the proclamation began, and that similarly the eschatological event has already begun with the proclaiming of the Gospel. Likewise, the baptized in the pentecostal community, and especially the apostle who now has the burden of bearing the proclamation, still feel the encouragement which the parable imparts. For the sake of this encouragement, tradition has preserved it.

2.

The second parable is joined to the first through the concise expression "and he said." Such editorial formulas customarily betray the hand of the writer, but they also show the pains taken to bind the two pieces together as closely as possible. Exegesis must take note of that.

Mᴋ. 4, 26–29:
26 The kingdom of God is as if a man should scatter seed upon the ground, [27]and should sleep and rise night and day, and the seed should sprout and grow, he knows not how. [28]The earth produces of itself, first the blade, then the ear, then the full grain in the ear. [29]But when the grain is ripe, at once he puts in the sickle, because the harvest has come.

The subject matter of this parable corresponds to a great extent to that of the first. There is the seed and the work of the sower, the fruitful earth, the increase of the seed, and the happy harvest.

But the stress is different, the tale has a different pivot. It says with emphasis that man does indeed throw out the seed, but he has nothing further to do with it. The impression is that he is completely idle; sleeping and rising again (and what is meant by that—waiting) seem the only thing to report. But in the meantime the seed grows up and one sees how the blade sprouts up, the ears appear, the grain in the ears grows full and firm. What must be understood by this, what constitutes the pivot of the parable, is stated in a pithy phrase: the earth creates all this "of itself," she has no need of man; he has no idea what is happening.

If the parable is placed in the situation of the beginning of Jesus' public life, and if it is assumed that amid all the disparity of structure there is an assertion similar to that of the first parable, then a meaning becomes clear. The preacher is relieved of an anxiety which is beyond human power to bear. What is begun there he need not bring to success; his affair is only to go through the land and, as he is charged, to deliver the tidings (cf. Mk. 1, 38). The working strength lies in the Gospel itself; the word proceeding from God is irresistible; it produces salvation or it leads to judgment.

3.

Mk. 4, 30–32:

30 With what can we compare the kingdom of God, or what parable shall we use for it? [31]It is like a grain of mustard seed, which, when sown upon the ground, is the smallest of all the seeds on earth; [32]yet when it is sown it grows up and becomes the greatest of all shrubs, and puts forth large branches, so that the birds of the air can make nests in its shade.

Here we see a manner of presentation which characterizes the structure of many parables: contrast. The grain of seed from the mustard shrub, proverbial for its tininess, stands in contrast to the developed plant which is called the largest of the garden plants.[9] It is important to note here that the contrast lies along the line of extension of time, in the opposition of Now and Then. There was, of course, also a definite contrast in the parable of the sowing: the success stood opposite the failure. But there the things opposed existed at the same time; it was, in fact, the one same course of work which brought forth the different results.[10] What we might call a spatial contrast, one in which the objects lie alongside one another, cannot direct attention to the future. It is different with the temporal contrast, the contrast of Now and Then. A parable using this method immediately calls up the fundamental theme of the Gospel. Thus this type alone should be called the "contrast-parable."

An example is here before us. The contrast between the grain of seed and the grown bush lies in the extension of time. It is also pertinent that the relation of Now and Then turns the attention towards the eschatological event. Yet, if one were content with only this contrast in the parable, or if the contrast were not to be understood as the tale presents it, or if what is said there so expressly and clearly with a purpose were to remain unnoted, then the question of the precise meaning of the discourse would have to remain unsettled. It is worthwhile, therefore, to look more closely.

The parable of the mustard seed is found in Luke's Gospel in a different position (13, 19–21), in an independent passage which probably stems from the sayings of Jesus.[11] There the mustard-seed parable is bound with that of the leaven in the manner of a double parable. The two have the same structure and the same introduction, and it is probable that they also have the same

25

theme. While the transcription appearing in Mark has separated the first of these, obviously because it speaks of a seed, and taken it over into the triple-group, in Matthew it has remained in that other context which preserves the double passage. Matthew has, of course, assimilated the textform of the first, which is from Mark, but he has not renounced the second. Whether we are concerned now with a genuine double parable or with a subsequent structuring of two independent passages,[12] the structure of the two is, in any case, so similarly laid out that one is able to shed light on the other.

The second parable (Lk. 13, 20f., or Mt. 13, 33[Q], says:

> To what shall I compare the kingdom of God? It is like leaven which a woman took and hid in three measures of meal, till it was all leavened.

If one were to discover here only a presentation of the contrast between beginning and end, and not to see that it is the all-embracing strength of the leaven that is spoken of—the "all" that is here spoken of is in fact that enormous quantity of more than 100 pounds of flour, and in a Jewish house only enough for one day is baked at a time—then one would obviously not do justice to the wording of the text. The phenomenon of an efficacy which must have appeared almost miraculous to the understanding of that time is here made into a parable. The story moves towards this point.[13]

To be sure, the view is obstructed if, misled by the introductory formulas, one understands the relation of the parabolical statement to the specified theme too narrowly. It need not be the Kingdom of God itself which succeeds and proves its strength there; it is sufficient for the meaning of the introduction if something connected with it is discussed. The parable does not at all necessitate seeking an object which is first small and invisible and in the end large and mighty. One need not, and one should not, say, for example, that the community of disciples is promised a mighty growth. It remains much closer to the way of thinking of the Gospel to imagine not a thing but a happening which reaches out around itself and gains strength.

These things must now be applied to the parable of the mustard seed. It speaks in another manner, of course; it does not lay the same full stress on the growth of the kernel as that of the leaven does on its working, but the parallelism does suffice to exclude an absolute, a completely unconnected contrast between mustard seed and bush. The great growth in which the birds dwell does not suddenly appear there, but it originated in the kernel. It is expressly said: "when it is sown *it grows up* and becomes the greatest of all shrubs. . . ."

Certainly, the presentation of this growth is disturbing if one decides beforehand that the eschatological event is here spoken of directly and without nuance. For, needless to say, this event knows no growth and no increase; it breaks in and with its irresistible force brings to completion that which was begun in the preliminaries of earthly events. But there is something else that can grow and increase and prove its transforming power: the Gospel, the word that enkindles a movement and presses irresistibly to its goal because it bears within itself the power of God. Here not only is the end considered, but the beginning is evaluated in terms of this end. Measured by worldly standards, the Gospel is indeed invisible; it is a message which cannot compel a hearing by means of force—indeed, it is even said of its proclaimer that He rejected the use of worldly influence as a Satanic temptation (cf. Mt. 4, 1–10, or Lk. 4, 1–12[Q]). And yet the word which goes forth from God is stronger than any power of earth. The disciple must learn not to be led astray by its apparent weakness. In this he is helped by the parable, for it shows in an everyday example the strength of something which appears trifling to the inexperienced.

So, although each places the stress differently and makes its own special assertion, the three parables also appear to be a tight unity in their theme. As a possession handed on, they demonstrate unanimously the spirit which the public life of Jesus animated. They give and strengthen the disciples of later generations—just as they confirmed the first who took part in the works of Jesus—in the certainty in faith that the Gospel will make its own way. It is not the messenger who brings success, but the message—the second parable; the Gospel possesses no means of earthly power to provide a hearing for itself, yet, because God addresses man through it, it will demonstrate the wondrous power that lies within it—the third parable; and so, just as despite various mishaps the seed arrives at its goal—the first parable—the work will succeed, and what was then begun in toil and difficulty will reveal itself in the light of the last day.

4.

In the construction of the fourth chapter of Mark there is joined to the first parable an exegesis (vv. 14–20) with its own introduction (vv. 10–13) and a concluding series of aphorisms (vv. 21–25). All this intrudes between the first and second parable and drives the formally and thematically closed structure apart. Thus it must be kept in mind that a meaningful working out and application of the parable found in earlier traditional material—

it might perhaps tentatively and in anticipation be called a sermon on the parable—is joined to the pertinent passage in the original text. But the piece is to be considered and treated first of all for its own sake.

v. 14: The sower sows the word.

This brief and clear sentence suits the meaning of the parable exactly. It could serve as a key sentence; we may even ponder whether it may not contain in itself a part of the original application. Moreover, the nearness to the parable is striking: where in the parable the sower was only a marginal figure whose mention belonged to the exposition—in contrast to the incident of the sowing the genuine tale began "and as he sowed" (v. 2)—so here, too, it is not said who the sower is, but only what is sowed. What is important is the message of Jesus, the proclamation of the dominion of God which has drawn near. The expression used here belongs to the early Christian vocabulary; the Gospel is simply "the word." The Acts of the Apostles, the letters of Paul, the First Letter of Peter, the first of John, that of James, and in Mark himself a series of marginal notes written by the evangelist all refer to it in this way.[14] If the early Christian preaching thus betrays itself in the vocabulary, it would appear so much the more amazing if the figure of the sower were to be renounced in the interpretation suggested. For this is after all no gratuitous pleasantry, but a meaning bound to a parable, following its structure. From this first definition, which tells what the seed and thus the sowing represent, the further details of the parable are now explained.

v. 15: And these are the ones along the path, where the word is sown; when they hear, Satan immediately comes and takes away the word which is sown in them.

Here the metaphor is completed: the word is sowed. But one compares these labored expressions—"and these are the ones along the path," "where the word is sown"—with the clear speech of the parable. The interpretation obviously attempts to stay as close as possible to the text.

> v. 16: And these in like manner are the ones sown upon rocky ground, who, when they hear the word, immediately receive it with joy; [17]and they have no root in themselves, but endure for a while; then, when tribulation or persecution arises on account of the word, immediately they fall away.

Certainly, Jesus, on the basis of His own experience, spoke to His disciples about oppression and persecution, but those words belong to a later phase of His public life, whereas the parable seems associated with its beginning. That many a man will be mistaken about the Gospel and falsely imagine that a life governed by this promise and the fate of a disciple in the world are easy, appears familiar to early Christian experience. Finally, the characterization of the fickle, who prove to be rootless and short-lived, indicates that this and the following passages attempt to show different ways of human refusal. It is to just this point that the interest of the admonishing sermon is directed.

> v. 18: And others are the ones sown among thorns; they are those who hear the word, [19]but the cares of the world, and the delight in riches, and the desire for other things, enter in and choke the word, and it proves unfruitful.

Certainly, the anxious cares of the Master echo here. The danger points which He himself repeatedly noted are clearly named: He spoke of the care for food and clothing—and through that of all the things of earthly existence—and demanded that that anxiety which abides in the depth of being be directed to no other good than the coming kingdom (Mt. 6, 24–33). He warned of riches (Mt. 6, 19–21; Lk. 12, 15–21). Words of the Lord can even be cited against "the desire for other things," perhaps for power and respect, but the expression is probably not intended so precisely. In any case it is seen that a life according to the Gospel is not compatible with concern for earthly stability and a desire for the deceptive security which riches offer. Whoever does not make this decision will remain "unfruitful" and thus not be able to pass through the tribunal of God.

> v. 20: But those that were sown upon the good soil are the ones who hear the word and accept it and bear fruit, thirtyfold and sixtyfold and a hundredfold.

It is striking how little the interpretation of this passage, which bears the main weight of the parable, has added. It repeats the text and adds only—in conformity with the opening phrase (v. 14)—the expression "who hear the word and accept it." Even the "bear fruit" is no longer interpreted. Perhaps the more highly developed parallel in Luke (8, 15) shows what has happened here. The "good soil" is now elucidated as the "honest and good heart" which holds to the word, endures, and brings forth its fruit. That the meaning of the last part is still so pale and indeterminate in Matthew shows that the interest of the sermon was not originally directed to it. Even more important is the urgency with which those details of the parable which speak of the perishing of the seed are handled. The question then arises how this emphasis came about and how it is related to the parable.

It has preserved the theme of the parable.[15] It has the Gospel in mind, although the over-all theme of this stage of the proclamation is already concentrated on the Christ figure. It sticks with the given text. It does not make the parable over completely into an allegory, that is into a figurative speech which is so built that every figure and every incident in it bears its own meaning. It does not seek to set up a deeper meaning beyond the literal meaning, which would correspond to allegory. So one must ask what really is the point of view from which in certain passages it completes the parable in allegorizing ways. For it does slight the concluding part, on which the weight of the parable lay, and turns to those details of the story which describe how the seed is ruined in various ways.

What does this mean? What was encouragement in one text has become a warning. What the little circle of the first disciples needed in order not to despair in the beginning situation is, of course, also needed by the early Christian community—it is for these Christians that the group of three parables of encouragement is transmitted; but something beyond that is necessary. Those who have received the Gospel, and in a special manner those who have newly entered the community, who must first learn to open themselves to it completely and to give it place in their own being, are admonishingly shown the many ways in which they could lose their discipleship. How the Gospel can perish within a man is pictured for them. Such a change of emphasis and mutation of the parable's assertion is possible because nothing is said in the warning which is not to be found expressly stated in the transmitted words of the Lord. One need only think of the warning passage of Jesus: "Every one then who hears these words of mine and does them will be like a wise man who built his house upon the rock. . . . And every one who hears these words of mine and does not do them will be like a foolish man who built his house upon the sand . . ." (Mt. 7, 24ff.).

That this suits the purpose of the passage is shown by the subsequent text. Having been taken into the composition and placed between the first and second parables, the passage must certainly be bound up with the chain of aphorisms which follows in verses 21–25. One can, therefore, imagine, if one supposes a sermon topic, that the explanation follows upon the reading of the parable and then its warning exhortation is fortified through a series of the Lord's statements. A first group of such sentences (vv. 21–23) states that the obscure must become as urgently apparent as the light must shine. In the given context that means: the proclamation which reveals God's plan of salvation can no longer be silent; it presses forward with the force of the inevitable. The second group (vv. 24–25) speaks vigorously of listening to this proclamation: "Take heed what you hear; the measure you give will be the measure you get, and still more will be given you." Then a warning sentence: "For to him who has will more be given; and from him who has not, even what he has will be taken away." The first group, therefore, goes back to the theme of the parable; the second, on the other hand, taking up the theme of the explanation, directs itself to the hearers: they should absorb whatever is possible for them to absorb: "Take heed what [that is, how much] you hear!" The measure of what has been absorbed, and thus the intensity of their eagerness, decides salvation and damnation.

5.

The composition is closed with a basic observation on the meaning of the parable discourse (4, 33–34). A comparison with the corresponding text in Matthew is extremely informative. Matthew tells us (13, 34–35):

34 All this Jesus said to the crowds in parables; indeed he said nothing to them without a parable. [35]This was to fulfill what was spoken by the prophet:
"I will open my mouth in parables,
I will utter what has been hidden since the foundation of the world."

Quoting from the prophets strengthens this declaration: Jesus' parable discourse serves to make the things of God comprehensible, not just for a narrow circle, but rather for the "crowd," for all in Israel who listen to the message. Originally the text of Mark (vv. 33–34), apart from the quoting of the prophets, says the same thing:

With many such parables he spoke the word to them,
    as they were able to hear it;
he did not speak to them without a parable.

In contrasting parallels, and with the emphasis of a double statement, speaking in parables is explained, therefore, as a sign of the friendliness with which Jesus preached to the people. He accommodated Himself to their understanding: "as they were able to hear it."

But now Mark makes an addition to the words "he did not speak to them without a parable." He says, "but privately to his own disciples he explained everything" (v. 34[b]). With this the meaning of the entire sentence is at once changed. Now he tells us that Jesus spoke to the people "merely" in parables. And the phrase "as they were able to hear it" now means that they were not able to grasp more than the external form and a certain obvious meaning of the discourse. The word *"parabolé"* has now no

34

longer the precise meaning of "parable" or "simile" but—and this is possible in the breadth of the Hebraic concept of "*mashal*"—the meaning of "enigma." The riddle needs a solution; its depths of meaning are disclosed only through interpretation, and the interpretation is given only to the disciples.

What Mark has done here is understandable. He has, in contrast to Matthew, adapted the concluding remarks on the parable discourse to what he had already said earlier where the explanation is joined onto the first parable. Probably he had previously found a version which said very simply that the disciples had asked Jesus about the meaning of the parable—perhaps just as we read it in Lk. 8, 9: "And when his disciples asked him what this parable meant,"—whereupon the explanation follows. Mark appears to have brought to this passage a theological theme which was important to him: the powerlessness of the human being to comprehend the secrets of God. This is true first of all of the disciples. To them it was said: "Do you not understand this parable? How then will you understand all the parables?" If one recalls how Mark later places each of the three forewarnings of the passion against the dark background of human folly—at the first Peter raises a protest (8, 32f.), upon the second follows the struggle of the disciples for rank (9, 33ff.), and upon the third the foolish proposition of the sons of Zebedee (10, 35ff.)—his intention becomes clear.

It is said of the disciples that of themselves they were not capable of understanding the parables; even they had need of the unique teacher. Now, the same theme appears on a second level: the mystery, which is called the kingdom of God, is graciously held out to the disciples. But to all who stand outside the circle of the disciples, the "parables" in the sense of comparisons turn to "parables" in the sense of inaccessible riddles.[16] The passage can be understood by an analysis of the literary structure. A statement of the Lord that probably belongs in the last phase of the prophetic battle of Jesus is here added on and strengthened through a citation of the prophets. The statement of the Lord says: "To you has been given the secret of the kingdom of God, but for those outside everything is in parables" (v. 11). If the two amplifications which Mark probably has applied to the text before him are placed together, they show that, completely unlike the situation of the early public life of Jesus, an inner place of discipleship is defined. Here already the reality of the Church stands in the consciousness. She is the called and accepted people to whom God has revealed His secret. The disciples possess no higher insight than those outside, but they have the single teacher and hear His word, which discloses the mysteries to them. If one considers that Mark wrote at a time in which the loosening of the Church from the old community of Israel was in full swing, then the vehemence of his theological presentation becomes comprehensible.

In the concluding commentary as it is contained in Matthew and in the form inflected by Mark, then, there are seen two differing interpretations of the parable discourse. There is apparently an older way of thinking that is closer to the words of Jesus, and therefore takes precedence, which in principle sees in the parable a means of understanding, spoken out of the desire to unlock the truth for the hearers, to provide them an access to the meaning, to convince and win them. Alongside, a later and secondary interpretation appears; it is probably determined by the late Jewish exegetical method, which accepted a multiple meaning and was inclined to see the real revelation in that very meaning which was not evident but concealed behind the verbal statement.

* * *

From the preceding observation, which had to be made on the three parables as well as on the meaning of the first, and also on the fundamental explanations of the function of the parable discourse, a few aspects should be kept in mind for further exegesis.

1) It is to be taken for granted of each parable, so long as no contrary evidence presents itself, that it has an exact, unequivocal meaning to be grasped in a single statement, which was recognizable at least to the original hearers. This meaning is easy to identify if the key that determines its significance is transmitted in convincing association with the parable in its introduction or application. Where such a word is lacking, or it must perhaps be conjectured that it is broken off and another word has been substituted for it, an attempt must be made to rediscover the original situation and to understand the parable according to the function which it could have had in this situation. That will sometimes be an external situation which can be recognized at least in its rough features from the synoptic presentation, but it is also worth-while in each case to ask about what we might call the "inner situation"—the place of the single discourse in the entire proclamation of Jesus.

2) But it is to be expected that another kind of interpretation of the parable discourse has also had its effect upon the transcription. In what way and to what extent this has happened must be observed in each individual case. But it can already be said that a meaning attached to a parable that attempts to go beyond what the key will bear is to be considered very carefully.

Such a meaning—and here we anticipate—need not by any means be separate from the parable. It can have penetrated even into the discourse itself in such a manner that it illuminates the individual details of the tale and challenges the hearers, by following its directions, to see the parable in a new and different light. The problem then presents itself of separating out, with discretion, the original speech, the words of Jesus, still not yet grasped and interpreted. It will be shown that in most cases a more or less certain knowledge can be attained, and this of course is true because the synoptic transcription, even there where it attempts to suggest an "other," an "allegorical" understanding, has preserved the basic text with fidelity.

3) If the parable theory of Mark is placed alongside the example of a deeper disclosure of meaning to which the context undoubtedly points—to be precise, the explanation of the first parable—then a discrepancy comes to light. The explanation does not at all attempt to discover within the parable a meaning which must remain obscure to the uninitiated. What it says in its own way lies on the same plane as the parable itself; what it teaches is to be grasped from a different, but not a higher, point of view. It is concerned with making the parable fruitful in a wise and effective manner for the broad circle of faithful in the community who are not in the role of proclaimers but of hearers. But nothing more is either achieved or even sought. So the interpretation which understands the parable as a cryptic speech must for the time being rest its case until more appropriate examples are found. But the tension which endures between the theological statement of the evangelist, at base a statement on the essence of revelation which would be worthy of John, and the specimen

which should afford an example, is pregnant in meaning. It makes us conscious of how strongly the early proclaimers and teachers felt themselves bound to the original words of the Lord, and how limited the leeway was for that which they themselves wished to say.

II.

The Messianic Age

The parables of the first group have attested to the efficacy of the Gospel which Jesus must proclaim. The "gospel" is a message which God himself sends; God does not merely stand behind it, as behind any teaching which imparts His truth and therefore occurs in His name. In the Gospel he speaks His own word as He did only once before in the divine language mediated by the prophets. After a long period of silence, in which one had only the holy Scriptures from the ancient times and the exegesis of the scholars to hold on to, and during which some pious people felt with anxiety and grief that "the spirit was quenched in Israel," He speaks now anew—reason enough to speak of a new age. But even that which the prophetic message announces is new, and those who hear it are ecstatic with wonder and amazement: "A great prophet has arisen among us! God has visited his people!" (Lk. 7, 16; cf. Mk. 1, 22. 27). So we must ask what the message says, what in it is new and not heard before, and what the meaning is of that which is now proclaimed. First of all, it must be observed that those originally addressed were in a different situation than a large part of today's hearers of the Gospel. Whether they feared or hoped for it, the coming event stood fast in their expectation: God will one day come forth out of His reserve full of power; through His tribunal He will conclude the earthly history effected and endured by men and introduce a new era

40

which is determined by His unbroken dominion, which will liberate creation to fulfill itself. This coming of the kingdom of God is a basic truth which Jesus did not proclaim as new, but presented as known.[17] So it must be asked again what is "new" in His message. The answer is found in the first place in the preaching of the Baptist. It forcefully sets in motion the movement which is taken up and carried further in the proclamation of Jesus. And this is what is new in the message to Israel: the awaited event is immediately at hand. John speaks as a prophet of doom; he startles men with the threat of the judgment: "Even now the axe is laid to the root of the trees; every tree therefore that does not bear good fruit is cut down and thrown into the fire" (Mt. 3, 10). Out of the threat comes the call to penance.

The reports belonging to the oldest layers of tradition (Mt. 3, 7-12; Lk. 3, 7-18[Q]) make clear that the prophetic vision is captivated by the Final Events. Even the messianic form which appears there stands stark in this connection: "His winnowing fork is in his hand, and he will clear his threshing floor and gather his wheat into the granary, but the chaff he will burn with unquenchable fire" (Mt. 3, 12; Lk. 3, 17). It can be said, therefore, that in this broad span in which the Now is bound with the most distant Then without any intermediate stage, in a manner characteristic of the prophetic viewpoint, there appears now the figure of Jesus, His public life, and the situation called forth by this public life.[18]

To announce the judgment and to call to conversion is the commission of Jesus, as it was that of the Baptist; a long series of parables will demonstrate that. But His proclamation reaches out far beyond that of the Baptist. Where the Baptist has, so to speak, provided the frame, Jesus now places within it the picture.

With this the special factor that tradition includes in the word "gospel" comes to the fore. The nearness of the kingdom of God is now perceptible for those who are able to see. The eschatological event is no longer sealed up in the absolute future; it no longer determines the future as pure threat, nor makes it bearable through expectation as pure promise; rather, it works within it and changes all relationships. A new situation has arisen, another time has come, and things happen which are not to be compared with the old works of God.

The consciousness of such "fullness of time" is still reflected in individual parables. They are few, but it can be presumed that there were many more of their sort. The two examined here were obviously preserved by tradition because they were incorporated in an already existing series of texts which belonged to the proclamation endowment of the community.

1.

The first is found in the long series of passages concerning the downfall of Jerusalem and, beyond it, the foreboding event of the Last Day. In Mk. 13, 28f., we find the text:

28 From the fig tree learn its lesson: as soon as its branch becomes tender and puts forth its leaves, you know that summer is near. 29So also, when you see these things taking place, you know that he is near, at the very gates.

A careful observation of the complex in which the parable occurs makes clear that although in its own way it does contribute to the sense of the whole, it does not fit well into the flow of thought. The text which precedes it (vv. 24–27), speaks already of the high point of the last events, the appearance of the Son of

Man; the parable, on the other hand, is obviously looking at the situation before the last crisis sets in and wishes to act as a warning on how to recognize its early omens.[19]

And so because the literary composition certainly occurred earlier, it can be asked where this passage really belongs, in which situation it was originally spoken. For we must at least reckon with the possibility that it belongs in the initial period, the time which has appropriately been named the "Galilean spring." If the text is considered under this hypothesis, an illuminating meaning is revealed.

The fig tree becomes a metaphor. In contrast to the other trees of Palestine—the olive tree, the evergreen oak, the carob tree—it loses its leaves in winter. So, with its fresh green it becomes a herald of the summertime. So also, the text now declares, the hearers of the message should know that "he" stands before the door—that is, the great, auspicious event. The parallel text in Luke (21, 31), in replacing the indefinite "he" with "the kingdom of God," gives the verse clarity; probably Luke's version here hits upon what was said originally and softened for the sake of the literary composition. The nearness of the kingdom is now to be recognized by the occurrence of "all this," of what is comparable to the promising green of the fig tree. This comparison suggests that the hearers think not of the fearful signs of that last crisis, but of the encouraging signs which accompany the Gospel. "These things" refers then to the same thing that another text out of that happy time has in mind: "But blessed are your eyes, for they see, and your ears, for they hear. Truly, I say to you, many prophets and righteous men longed to see what you see, and did not see it, and to hear what you hear, and did not hear it" (Mt. 13, 16f.; Lk. 10, 23f.[Q]).

The initial period, perhaps more exactly the period of the first encounters with the authorities of Israel, could be the original setting for the conversation in which a few from the circle of Pharisees ask Jesus when the kingdom of God will come; —the question may be asked seriously, for it corresponds to the "apocalyptic" way of thinking of some circles in Judaism. Jesus declines the question and yet does give an answer: "The kingdom of God is not coming with signs to be observed; nor will they say, 'Lo, here it is!' or 'There!'; for behold, the kingdom of God is in the midst of you" (Lk. 17, 20f.).[20] So different is its coming, so different is its declaration, so seriously must its efficacious nearness be taken, that every look into the future is fruitless if it is not able to recognize what already stands before its eyes.

A second verse belongs to this: "But if it is by the Spirit of God that I cast out demons, then the kingdom of God has come upon you" (Mt. 12, 28; Lk. 11, 20[Q]).

To attempt to read into these texts that the eschatological expectation is abandoned and that simply the presence of the kingdom of God is explained, would be to misunderstand the style of speech. In it there is expressed the recognition that present and future have entered into a new, intensively reciprocal relationship. That which is to come has already deeply affected the present events, has opened up the present to its influence; the present is already permeated with the very reality of that which is to come. Thus there arise genuine prefigurations of that which in the end will be disclosed; salvation comes to pass, and the awakening of the dead and liberation from the enslaving might of the adversary. Forgiveness and reconciliation and a new freedom will never die. The will of God will become more clearly and more penetratingly manifest, and a bolder certainty of His love will be discovered and a new courage will be awakened to follow this love.

This is the situation which has arisen with the appearance of Jesus. It can be designated first of all with an expression which was given it already in the Jewish tradition: the messianic age. The expression is useful because in the official teaching of Judaism the figure of the Messiah as such was not exalted. He is seen not as an effector but only as a representative, not as the epitome but as a sign of recognition of the awaited time of salvation.[21]

Between this understanding and the way of thinking of Jesus there exists a strange sort of correspondence, whatever the basis for it might be. He speaks with vigor of the time which is now come and of the situation which has arisen, but He does not proclaim the Messiah. With composure and patience He allows a long development so that of itself there might arise the question: which attitude towards the prophetic commission is imparted by the words of God themselves? He grants the time for an entirely new insight to ripen before it finally comes to the surface. On the other hand, He demands from the very beginning that one be able to "interpret the present time" (cf. Lk. 12, 54–56), and He speaks of that which is required with full prophetic power.

The parables to be reviewed in this section therefore belong for thematic reasons close to those of the first group. The new message and the new situation stand alongside one another. And both are bound to the figure of Jesus.

2.

A spare but expressive parable is found in the complex of Mk. 2, 18–22:

18 Now John's disciples and the Pharisees were fasting; and people came and said to him, "Why do John's disciples and the disciples of the Pharisees fast, but your disciples do not fast?" [19]And Jesus said to them, "Can the wedding guests fast while the bridegroom is with them? As long as they have the bridegroom with them, they cannot fast. [20]The days will come, when the bridegroom is taken away from them, and then they will fast in that day. [21]No one sews a piece of unshrunk cloth on an old garment; if he does, the patch tears away from it, the new from the old, and a worse tear is made. [22]And no one puts new wine into old wineskins; if he does, the wine will burst the skins, and the wine is lost, and so are the skins; but new wine is for fresh skins."

The material in verses 18–19 forms a tight unity: Jesus is asked a question and He answers by using a teaching method which was also in practice among the rabbis—that is to say, with a counter-question. But the counter-question not only makes it necessary for the interrogator himself also to recall the answer (cf., for example, Lk. 10, 26); here it offers him a parable which through the power of its logic helps him to perception. But the parable is hindered in its development because it is completely absorbed in the counter-question to which its form is subordinated. Were it able to develop, perhaps it would say: a father of a house held a wedding for his son; the guests came, but they did not wish to eat and be merry. Then the father said to them: Can the wedding guests fast. . . . Instead of this, the point of the story is reached immediately without any preliminaries.

The meaning of the text is yielded first of all by the question which was to be answered. It was asked why the disciples of Jesus did not observe the pious practice of the twice a week fast. That this was pointed towards the piety of the Pharisees, but above all and more essentially towards the penitential seriousness of the disciples of John, is obvious. Behind it stands the com-

46

parison which was also drawn between the kind of life of Jesus and that of the Baptist: "For John came neither eating nor drinking, and they say, 'He has a demon': the Son of man came eating and drinking, and they say, 'Behold, a glutton and a drunkard, a friend of tax collectors and sinners!'" (Mt. 11, 18–19). What here developed even to reviling Jesus enters first of all only as an astonished but still innocent question. It is incomprehensible that Jesus and His circle do not manifest the seriousness of piety as it is learned from the authoritative teachers, but above all from the venerated prophet John. This question Jesus now answers.

The parable is self-explanatory; for the pictures of the messianic time of joy are confided to all who hear it. The difficulty lies elsewhere. The parable has value only if it is acknowledged beforehand that the time of salvation is now really begun. A parable which serves this proclamation and carries in itself its claim, which is illuminating to some and obscuring to others, can only strengthen the response to the Gospel itself: joyful certitude by the one, gloomy resignation or sharp vexation with the other. But this in any case is clear: the adoration of God which arises in freedom is in conformity with the situation which has newly arisen, and a life in joy and confidence means a witness to its truth.

This piece, too, is of course preserved undamaged in the early Christian proclamation, but explained through supplements and prepared for the use of the community. There is first of all the double text of verses 21–22. It works by a comparison: as new, still unshrunken cloth does not fit well with old cloth, as old inelastic skins are not well-suited to new wine, so generally the new does not go well with the old; it should be left to itself. As the wisdom of this passage can be applied broadly, it can scarcely be said on what occasion it was originally spoken. But tradition has annexed it as a concluding statement to the parable of the wedding. Here it strengthens the assertion that the time which is now come demands something other than penance and mourning. That does not mean that the disciples are now forbidden to fast; it is not concerned with replacing an established duty with a new one. It is much more concerned with freedom. When His disciples and along with them He himself are called to account on their way of life or even criticized (as, for example, in Mk. 2, 23), then Jesus answers with a sharpness that goes to the principle of the matter.

What is said in verse 20 remains to be considered. The verse is introduced with a "but" which is not merely transitional but consciously contrastive; it therefore limits what was said before. The picture of the joyful wedding is now displaced by the description of a catastrophe: the bridegroom is forcibly abducted, and the troubled guests fall into a sadness in which they can no longer feast.

It might be supposed that another allegorical wedding passage from a different time, perhaps the last phase of the messianic conflict, has been quoted in the composition.[22] But what does that mean for the original parable? Here the focus was on the wedding feast; at such a celebration one cannot fast. But now the figure of the bridegroom is removed; the situation of the wedding retreats to the background; the bride, who is, after all, the most hurt, is now not even mentioned; the talk is only of the guests who grieve over the loss of the bridegroom. What has happened here is clear: in the figure of the bridegroom was discovered a representation of Jesus; in His passion He is taken from His friends. Thus the structure of the parable is altered by a single

48

sentence. The salient point is moved from the tale to the second wedding text. Now catastrophe and sorrow stand in focus. So, although the wording of the parable is maintained, its assertion has receded. And with this shift the double text of the old and the new (vv. 21f.), which probably had already been joined to the parable much earlier and had acted to confirm the parable's assertion, has become as it were unattached.

In contrast to the parable, the passage of the abducted bridegroom is a late text and its connection a probably still later occurrence. It is evident that here the early Christian proclamation has been at work. In seeking the motive, it should be noted first of all that a basis is needed for the continuation of the Jewish custom of fasting in the community of disciples, in apparent opposition to the directions of the parable. Moreover, it is at least suggested that this fast is directed towards something other than that of the Jews: it is not profitable works of penance which should be performed; rather, the pain over the fate of the Master finds its expression here.

But another stronger and more preëminent motive seems to have been the cause. The early Christian sermon had as its central theme the death and the messianic glorification of Jesus. To die was the great task that the Messiah had to fulfill according to God's decree, and the glorification had founded what might be called the Easter life of the community of disciples. Placed in power, the Messiah had filled them with his life through the bestowing of the Spirit, and the old covenant between God and Israel had been renewed and fulfilled. Now, removed to heaven, Jesus exchanged life and love with the community of His disciples. Thus the covenantal relationship of Yahweh to Israel had solidified and concretized itself, and thus it was possible to make the prophetic image of the marriage covenant fruitful for the proclamation. What was never stated of the Messiah—so far as it can be learned from the sources—in the Jewish sphere is now said by the sermon: the heavenly Lord is the bridegroom and the Church filled with His Spirit is the bride (cf. 2 Cor. 11, 2; Eph. 5, 25; Jn. 3, 29). It thus becomes comprehensible that a parable which speaks of a bridegroom and calls up the image of a wedding and a feast can scarcely be heard as anything but a self-revelation of the heavenly Lord. But then it will also be understandable why the passage of the shattered wedding has been quoted and why the stress of the parable has been shifted to the catastrophe. Now the discourse has been given a function similar to that of the triple announcement of the passion. It concludes significantly with the expression placed at the end: "in that day" (v. 20).

The double task given to exegesis is quite clear in this example. The distance between the speech of Jesus and that of the early Christian preaching is strikingly great. So it is worthwhile to treat the two separately. It has been said of preaching that it concentrates on its central theme and adapts the traditional parable for its own proclamation. It does this with discretion; it takes nothing away from the transmitted text, but satisfies its needs by means of the literary composition. That such a method is used at all has its basis, of course, in the fact that one is constrained to support one's own word with the word of the Lord as much as possible. Yet at the same time there is the other task made possible by the caution of tradition: to release the original text from the complex in which it occurs and to understand it as such. Perhaps it is now clear what we have to gain by our labors.

3.

The parables of the fig tree and of the wedding, as well as the passages on the kingdom of God which has already come and is in the midst of men, speak impressively of the situation which is announced and at the same time introduced by the preaching of the Baptist and the prophetic work of Jesus. The future event has now approached so near that its power penetrates the present from within. Its place of entrance is the Gospel, and the Gospel appears and reveals itself through the "accompanying signs" (Mk. 16, 17f.). But the signs are prophetic; they themselves do not bring to completion what only the work of the Last Day can produce, but they point to that work and fortify hope. The sufferers whom Jesus heals are not healed forever; those called back into life must die; those who have found forgiveness are tempted further. All, even the proclamation and the faith which it wakes, hold their ground only by toil, by struggle, by mortal combat. If, then, it is asserted that the kingdom exists in the present time, it can be understood in no other way than as dynamic: whatever of reality exists in the future of the Last Day now presses in and gains for itself a fore-presence which can never be separated from its actual entrance. So the old remains in power up till "that day." The preaching of the apostles states this clearly: the baptized belong already to the future; through them the new eon has begun to burst through the old. But they must live in "the present evil age" (Gal. 1, 4), and they endure "the sufferings of this present time" (Rom. 8, 18; cf. 2 Cor. 4, 16–18). But that which became clear at the end, after all that happened with Jesus, was not necessarily so in the beginning. What Jesus says of the power which works in the Gospel and of

51

the situation which has newly arisen could easily become "secularized." As soon as the eschatological tension is forgotten, misunderstandings arise as though the return of Paradise were to be expected for this time. What is expected then no longer agrees with reality, and doubt and perhaps even vexation spring up.

A parable that belongs to the special matter of Matthew seems to us to fit into this context: that of the weeds in the field (13, 24–30). It demands a painstaking treatment.

24 The kingdom of heaven may be compared to a man who sowed good seed in his field; [25]but while men were sleeping, his enemy came and sowed weeds among the wheat, and went away. [26]So when the plants came up and bore grain, then the weeds appeared also. [27]And the servants of the householder came and said to him, "Sir, did you not sow good seed in your field? How then has it weeds?" [28]He said to them, "An enemy has done this." The servants said to him, "Then do you want us to go and gather them?" [29]But he said, "No; lest in gathering the weeds you root up the wheat along with them. [30]Let both grow together until the harvest; and at harvest time I will tell the reapers, Gather the weeds first and bind them in bundles to be burned, but gather the wheat into my barn."

First of all, a few observations. That this, like every genuine parable, concerns a "story from life" or at least a true-to-life story, can be shown by a folk tale from Palestine.[23] A poor farmer had let his cattle pasture on strange ground. The owner denounced him and he was punished. Now he tells how he took his revenge: "At the end of the summer I went down into the valley in which there is reed-grass, tall as a man and with seed panicles like chaff. I plucked the panicles until I had filled my cloak, drew the tips through the shoulder holes [of the armless cloak], . . . went to the field . . . which was freshly ploughed . . . and threw the seeds of reed-grass in. In less than a year it was thick with reed-grass. . . ."

How understandable now is the suspicion of the master of the house that the extraordinary thick stand of weeds in the field which was sown with the carefully sorted wheat grains comes from his enemy. The remark in verse 26 that the weeds are recognizable only at the onset of the harvest is explained by recalling the whirling darnel, which in the first stages of the blade's development can be mistaken for wheat. Its seeds are, in effect, poisonous for man; they spoil the flour.[24]

In verse 27 the question is raised whether the weeds should be torn out. That the question is sensible is demonstrated by the practice still in use today of weeding through the growing seed, even when the weeds stand thick. On the other side, there is good reason for the master of the house to say no; he may be apprehensive that the wheat, whose weaker roots are entwined in the stronger roots of the darnel, will be torn out along with them. At the harvest, however, the reapers should be directed not to take the darnel into the sheaves; it should be bundled and dried to serve later as fuel for fire.

The parable speaks of the kingdom of God. But that means, as has already so often been made clear, that it is speaking of something which is related to it. The allusion to the harvest reveals to us more precisely just what is under discussion. Already in the prophets the harvest is marked as an image for the judgment (as, for example in Jl. 4, 13; cf. also Mt. 3, 12), and such associations are interwoven in the choice of the subject and the imagery of the parables; so they, too, illuminate the meaning. The judgment thus stands in focus, but it does not constitute the real theme of the parable. The structure of the tale must be considered; it does not describe the episode of the harvest, as, for example, the parable of the fish net describes the sifting and separation of the catch (Mt. 13, 47ff.). Thus it does not make the events of the harvest present to the listener; it does not take place before his eyes—it is brought into view only indirectly, through the speech of the master of the house. On the other hand, the dialogue between the master and the servants stands in the present; it is in this dialogue that the structure has its focal point. What, then, happens in this dialogue? If we again observe the structure, a problem is uncovered and brought forth—the spoiled grain field, and a solution is suggested for it—weeding it out. But this suggestion is rejected: all is to be left as it is. In this decision lies the focal point of the dialogue, and along with it that of the parable. It refuses to solve the problem abruptly, and demands that it be suffered and borne until the solution is at last found.

Exegesis must therefore ask first of all whether the problem in the parable corresponds to a problem of the listeners—a problem, that is, which is experienced in the present but is not to be solved in the present. Such a problem can be identified. It was asked in an elemental fashion in the old and never silenced question of how God, who is indeed wise, powerful, and good, could permit the wicked to thrive and go their own way in this world unpunished. One remembers the torturing thoughts that run through the Book of Job, such as the meditation on the uninterrupted good fortune of the godless (21, 7–18), and places alongside it a text from the Psalter so familiar to Jesus' listeners. There the Psalmist asks (Ps. 10, 1–6):

Why dost thou stand afar off, O Lord?
　Why dost thou hide thyself in times of trouble?
In arrogance the wicked hotly pursue the poor;
　let them be caught in the schemes which they have devised.
For the wicked boasts of the desires of his heart,
　and the man greedy for gain curses and renounces the Lord.

In the pride of his countenance the wicked does not seek him;
  all his thoughts are, "There is no God."
His ways prosper at all times;
  thy judgments are on high, out of his sight;
  as for all his foes, he puffs at them.
He thinks in his heart, "I shall not be moved;
  throughout all generations I shall not meet adversity."

And the tormented acknowledges (Ps. 73, 2–4. 10–12):

But as for me, my feet had almost stumbled,
  my steps had well nigh slipped.
For I was envious of the arrogant,
  when I saw the prosperity of the wicked.
For they have no pangs;
  their bodies are sound and sleek. . . .
Therefore the people turn and praise them;
  and find no fault in them.
And they say, "How can God know?
  Is there knowledge in the Most High?"
Behold, these are the wicked;
  always at ease, they increase in riches.

What actually weighs on the God-fearing who speak here, and
drives them to the very brink of vexation and scandal, is not the
experience as such, but the fruitlessness of the expectation that
God will interfere and make the right prevail. The prosperity of
sinners, and in glaring contrast to this the multiple sorrows of
the pious, place a heavy burden on faith in the living God. That
the circle of acquaintances of Jesus thought so, too, is shown by
the disciples' question whether one ought not to pray that fire
from heaven might fall on the villages which refused hospitality
to the saints of God (Lk. 9, 51–56). The counterpart is visible,
too—the idea that God must and will defend the pious from
harm. "There were some present at that very time who told him
of the Galileans whose blood Pilate had mingled with their

sacrifices . . ." (Lk. 13, 1–5). One hears here how astonished and dismayed the people are and what questions torture them. In some cases it could be questioned whether those struck down were not in sin and were thereby judged, but these Galileans were on the temple grounds and were apprehended in the most sublime act of divine worship; yet God permitted them to be slaughtered at the same time as their victims.

The problem is old, but for those who believe the Gospel it has grown more difficult. For now, when the messianic age of rejoicing has come and the delivering power is everywhere at work, how should the misery of the God-fearing and the prosperity of the godless be understood? Must not just this very "sign" of the nearness of divine sovereignty be experienced before every other? Why is the power of Him who has come manifest only to the physically and spiritually sick and deformed, but not to the poor and suppressed? Is the time not now come to create justice in the world?

At bottom, there can be seen the same misunderstanding of the situation as exists on other levels concerning the fate of Jesus. Those who surmised or recognized the Messiah in Him were dominated by the idea that the Messiah would have at his disposal the unveiled power of God and therefore must succeed without flaw or crisis; —there comes to mind here the reprimand ventured by Peter after he heard the prophecy of the passion (Mk. 8, 32), or the demand of the sons of Zebedee for the places at the right and left of the enthroned (Mk. 10, 35ff.), or the indignation of the disciples about the rejection of Jesus in the district of the Samaritans (Lk. 9, 51ff.) and their question whether the procession to Jerusalem meant that now the kingdom of God would come or that the messianic dominion was now established for Israel (Acts 1, 6f.). Every time it is the same short circuit; it is not understood that the present events stand under a law other than that of eschatological fulfillment.

It is thus imaginable that the question about the condition of the world and justice was brought up to Jesus from within the circle of disciples. But the answer is not presented directly in a pedagogical pronouncement; it does not "settle" the question, but it "gives something to think about." The problem along with its working out is transposed into the parable. Whoever is able to hear learns from it that the decree of God works along lines other than the thoughts of man (Mk. 8, 33[b]), and recognizes the will of God: that this existence, threatened by injustice, marked by constantly new wrongs, is to be endured in the patience that comes from hope, in the strength which knowledge of the true God gives, in the incorruptibility which holds itself on the side of God and does not come to terms with human authority.

The parable and its assertion should be left in this breadth. It should not be narrowed, and above all it should not be removed from its basis, the plane of the created. Indeed, it cannot be strange that Jesus has eyes and ears for the state of the world and for the perplexed questions of the God-fearing. The tradition in which He stood had no inclination to lose sight of creation. It valued the Book of Genesis and everything from the Psalms and wisdom literature that were based upon it. Thus Jesus' preaching, too, spoke not only of the "deliverance of Israel," but also and much more of the deliverance and fulfillment of the created world. For just this reason the prophetic signs bear the character of healing, and the healing happens to those who, suffering physically and enslaved spiritually, are discarded with contempt and separated from the circle of the others. The sufferings of creatures are recognized and healed as such.

The significance of the parable would then be narrowed by attempting to find within it something like the answer to the demand for a "sinless community."[25] Doubtless, such thoughts had occurred in Israel, but it is improbable that they could have arisen in the company of Jesus. The narrower as well as the wider circle of his adherents had been formed in a completely different school of thought. Tradition states this with emphasis; we need only think of the report on the summoning of the tax collector Levi (Mk. 2, 13–17).

On the same basis, to seek in the midst of the community of disciples for the problem taken up in the parable of Jesus would be an error. Certainly, it also emerges later in an analogical fashion in the sphere of the Church in easily recognizable presuppositions; it might even be said to appear in several passages of the New Testament. But in the proclamation of Jesus it has no place.

4.

As in the case of Mark's telling of the sowing, a meaning is added to the parable of the weeds. Yet methodological reasons recommend that the parable of the catching of fish be examined first.

Mt. 13, 47–50:
47 Again, the kingdom of heaven is like a net which was thrown into the sea and gathered fish of every kind; 48when it was full, men drew it ashore and sat down and sorted the good into vessels but threw away the bad. 49So it will be at the close of the age. The angels will come out and separate the evil from the righteous, 50and throw them into the furnace of fire; there men will weep and gnash their teeth.

At the root lies a comparison: just as the fishers sort their catch, picking out and throwing away the worthless, so on the Last Day will the evildoers be sorted out and rejected.[26] But the tale which turns the comparison into a parable is already a considerably developed piece. One sees how the dragnet is tossed out from the rowboats and drawn on ropes through the water up to the land, how it comes out filled, and how the fishers sit themselves down and work over the catch. They take out what is inedible, crabs and other animals and what is defined as unclean, "fish without scales," "fish without fins," and so forth;[27] but what is good they place in vessels.

The elaboration of the comparison in the application (v. 49) makes clear that nothing but the sorting out of the catch should be taken into consideration. Of course, there is a great temptation to interpret the episode of the fish-catching, too, all the more so as a statement of the Lord has been handed down in which He told the disciples that they should be made "fishers of men" (Mk. 1, 17; cf. Lk. 5, 10). It might, then, in a parallel to the parable of the weeds, be said: Now the proclamation goes forth to all without differentiation, and everyone is invited to place himself among those who await Him who is to come; and it is not for Jesus, and still less for His disciples, to distinguish between genuine disciples and those who only bear the name, between the earnest and the frivolous, the really converted and those who have not changed at bottom. That belongs to the judgment of God alone, and the judgment occurs not now in the time of this world, but on the Last Day.[28] The interpretation could even go a step further and find the Church presented as the fish net in which the just and unjust exist alongside one another. In that case, the parable's warning would be understood as an admonishment to desist from "judging" (Mt. 7, 1) and to bear with the foolish and the lukewarm brethren and the sinners. But all that would not be true to the parable. The tale is built differently: those who haul out the net are indeed the same people who afterwards sort the catch, but it is only this latter point that is pertinent, for it is concerning it that the comparison is made.

So the simile of the net coincides with the last verse of the parable of the cockle. The correspondence is so exact that some writers wish to speak of a "double parable":[29] the fishers parallel the harvest workers, the hauling in of the net the mowing, the removal of the unusable catch the bundling and burning of the weeds. But if the entire parable of the cockle is placed alongside the parable of the net, then it can be seen how different the two pieces are. That of the catch of fish says only that in the end there will be a judgment. It serves as a threatening and warning speech in placing before our eyes the separation of the evildoers from the just and their rejection, just as in the story of the shepherd who separates the goats from the sheep (Mt. 25, 32). The parable of the weeds has another intention. It relates the future judgment to the present situation in order to illuminate this present. It does not serve as a warning or threat, but as an acknowledgment of the ways of God which makes it possible for us to live out our lives in trustful patience.

5.

It will now be easier to find a starting point for the interpretation of the parable of the weeds. The first thing to be considered is the place which Matthew has provided for it within the composition

of the thirteenth chapter, and that leads to the prior question of
how he has fitted the parable itself, which belongs to his own special materials, into the older composition of Mark. This much is
apparent: from the closed triple group of the seed parables he has
excluded the middle piece, that of the growing seed, and replaced
it by the parable of the weeds. There can be opinions on his mo-
tives, but anything certain is scarcely possible. We can be certain
only about the fact itself. But it is extraordinary that he has not
attached the interpretation directly to the parable. On the contrary, he begins by bringing forth the third of the group of three,
the parable of the mustard seed, and the parable closely connected
with it, that of the leaven (13, 31–33). He lets stand the concluding notes on the teaching methods of Jesus which follow in
Mark (13, 34), and then he begins anew and brings in as a kind
of supplement three further pieces from his special matter. Finally, he forms a fresh conclusion for the newly constructed complex with the passage which compares the scribe who is well-
trained in matters of the kingdom of God to a wise householder
(13, 51f.).

The interpretation of the parable of the weeds constitutes the
first piece of that supplement. It is therefore worth noting that,
unlike the treatment of the parable of the sowing in Mark's transmission, Matthew does not annex the interpretation immediately
to the parable of the weeds, but foregoes interrupting a second
time the composition which has meanwhile solidified. The un-
natural separation of parable and interpretation which arises was
perhaps tolerated because for Matthew the two pieces did not lie
on the same plane. This is only a conjecture, but it can incite us
to examine the interpretation more exactly.

Mt. 13, 36–43:

36 Then he left the crowds and went into the house. And his disciples came to him, saying, "Explain to us the parable of the weeds of the field." [37]He answered, "He who sows the good seed is the Son of man; [38]the field is the world, and the good seed means the sons of the kingdom; the weeds are the sons of the evil one, [39]and the enemy who sowed them is the devil; the harvest is the close of the age, and the reapers are angels.

40 Just as the weeds are gathered and burned with fire, so will it be at the close of the age. [41]The Son of man will send his angels, and they will gather out of his kingdom all causes of sin and all evildoers, [42]and throw them into the furnace of fire; there men will weep and gnash their teeth. [43]Then the righteous will shine like the sun in the kingdom of their Father. He who has ears, let him hear."

The two paragraphs quoted here are chiefly differentiated in their choice of words. The second works with verbs, the first places noun alongside noun. The change is determined by the method. Since the parable is to be interpreted in an allegorical manner, detail by detail, all the figures named there are first of all examined and defined and introduced as if in a list (vv. 37–39); and only then is the event disclosed (vv. 40–43). It is now worth asking in what way and from what point the entire explanation is obtained. Was the "list" there first and was the event of the harvest understood in relation to it; or did the act of defining all the figures in the parable tale result from a concretizing explanation of the harvest in an attempt at recapitulation?

Beyond that there is the following to observe: what is said in the second excerpt agrees in essentials with the parable of the net. The comparison which is drawn there is found again here almost verbatim: verse 40 = 49[a]: "So it will be at the close of the age"; verse 41 = 49[b]: the angels will be sent out to bring the evildoers together; verse 42 = 50: they will "throw them into the furnace of fire; there men will weep and gnash their teeth." But inasmuch as the parable of the net shows a closed structure—the parallel statement of verse 49f. belongs to the substance of this speech—it must be supposed that the interpretation of the harvest procedure is acquired from there.[30]

But the comparison also shows where the assertion of verses 40–43 about the material offered in the net parable is heading. There God himself was the Lord of the judgment. His name is not mentioned; His work appears in that of the serving angel. Thus it corresponds to the old kind of talk about God, which veils the holy name, but it also corresponds to Jesus' manner of speech and the thematic of the early proclamation. There He speaks not of Himself and His place in the event of salvation, but simply of God and of what *He* will do. Thus something new comes to the fore in the explanation of the parable: now instead of God it is the "Son of man" who exercises judgment; it is "His" angels who prepare and execute it; and His scope of dominion is the world.[31]

But if all this is true, then the explanation seems to belong to the same layer of tradition as the statement of the apostle Paul which says of the events of the Last Day: "Then comes the end, when he [Christ] delivers the kingdom of God the Father.... For he must reign until he has put all his enemies under his feet.... When all things are subjected to him, then the Son himself will also be subjected to him who put all things under him, that God may be everything to every one" (1 Cor. 15, 24–28). In line with this, then, the dominion of the Messiah is circumscribed by the deeper, all-confirming dominion of God, but the reverse is also true: as long as the time of this world endures, the dominion of God comes to light as the dominion of Jesus, who has been elevated and placed in power.

All the elements quoted in the "list" are subsequent results, according to this explanation of the harvest. It follows that when the evildoers are separated and annihilated in judgment, they are symbolized by the weeds. But in that case, the wheat represents the "sons of the kingdom."[32] Since the judgment happens to all peoples, the field must mean the "world," the entire inhabited earth.[33] And because in the parable the lord of the house who has sowed the seed is the same one who in the end gathers the harvest, the Son of man is seen already in the sower. From there on, the faithful can again be interpreted as His good seed, and likewise the wicked as the seed of the devil.

If the meaning in its essentials (vv. 40–43) is gained from the parable of the net in such a manner, then something else becomes comprehensible. It may seem strange at first that this passage does not succeed in touching the salient point the parable wished to lay open. This point lay in the decision of the master of the house that the weeds should be left; the reference to the harvest stood throughout in second place, serving only to make the decision tolerable. In the explanation, on the other hand, the problem of the present situation seems to have vanished from sight, and all the interest seems to be centered upon the judgment proceedings. But the reason for this can be conjectured. The proclaimers of the Gospel were obviously completely infatuated with the theme of the final judgment. Their hope found support in this truth, and its description helped their preaching; for in such imagery the proclamation of the Messiah was intelligible to even the simplest souls.

How the proclamation elaborates such a theme can be shown by an example. In the speech of Peter in the Acts of the Apostles it is said that the Messiah Jesus, who returned to God, who was

64

clothed with the glory of God and was enthroned at the right hand of God (cf. Acts 2, 30–33), is He "whom heaven must receive until the time for establishing all that God spoke" (Acts 3, 21). That is now carried out in a way familiar to the Pauline communities: "The Lord Jesus is revealed from heaven with his mighty angels in flaming fire, inflicting vengeance upon those who do not know God" (2 Thes. 1, 7–10; cf. 1 Thes. 4, 16–17; 1 Cor. 15, 52).

But next to the parable's explanation stands the great description of the Last Judgment which Matthew himself, drawing upon his own special matter, made the concluding member of a chain of parables on the Second Coming (23, 27—25, 46). The passage begins with the words: "When the Son of man comes in his glory, and all the angels with him, then he will sit on his glorious throne. Before him will be gathered all the nations, and he will separate them one from another as a shepherd separates the sheep from the goats . . ." (25, 31–32). Our text gives the same image of judgment, but as it were on a smaller scale.

But we must here again observe how the proclamation has had an influence. After the text of the interpretation had already become fixed, the proclamation appears to have expanded the discourse once again. The explanation itself, obviously determined by the theme of the parable of the weeds, had only the rejection of the wicked in mind; it had in an amazing way refrained from allegorizing the act of bringing the wheat into the barn. But the later preaching needs a balanced picture of the judgment, a picture which contains the reception of the good as well as the rejection of the evil. So the explanation is left as it is, but is supplemented by a text on the salvation of the God-fearing, which must be taken as a free quotation from the Book of Daniel (12, 3). The discourse echoes it in its words of promise: "Then the righteous will shine like the sun in the kingdom of their Father" (v. 43).

If, after all these individual observations, the explanation is again placed alongside the original parable, it will perhaps be clear that the two lie on different planes. Certainly, the parable of Jesus then stands forth clearly in its own right, and its assertion is no longer under the threat of being restricted by an explanation which does not measure up to its stature. But justice is also due the early Christian proclamation. The care which it exercises, the perceptions which move it to make its own statements, the manner in which it treats the transmitted materials— all these must be appreciated. It is in no way concerned about explaining the parable in what we today would call an exegetical manner; it transmits it as it stands and uses it as a basis for preaching. But then, closely annexed to the word of the Lord, it expounds what it itself has to say. The freedom it claims in order to do this is not arbitrary, for it can say nothing but what is already said: it "produces" no new text, but out of the transmitted material of the Lord's words, which it understands in the light of the total proclamation of Jesus, it draws that which buttresses and supports its own assertion. It is in this bond with the materials of tradition that it appears to base its right to offer that which it says is the teaching of the Lord. The preaching which is to be perceived in all this has the rank of the inspired word as much as the proclamation which occurs in the letters of the apostles.

III.

The Warning to Israel

It is clear in the synoptic presentations, especially Mark's, that after the early period of prophetic activity, in which Jesus' message, because of its promises, was embraced by the people with eager expectations, a phase of strife with the authorities had begun. In the beginning, He had worked in Galilee, so that even in space His work stood apart from the authoritative persons and places. From the reports it can still be seen that only after some time, and indeed on the basis of accounts which came into Jerusalem, did the Pharisees begin to trouble themselves about the proceedings in Galilee (Mk. 3, 22; 7, 1; cf. Jn. 4, 1). Moreover, the meetings of Jesus with the spiritual leaders were certainly not burdened from the first with distrust and hostility. They, for their part, showed first of all an interest and a readiness for discussion, as is proper for genuine scholars. A few reports speak of invitations which Jesus received for dinner and with it for learned conversation (cf. Lk. 7, 36; 11, 37; 14, 1); such conversation need not have had a polemical bent. The discussion on the question of the great commandment reported by Mark (Mk. 12, 28–34) shows a friendly and earnest agreement. Even an exchange such as that at Simon's dinner party (Lk. 7, 36ff.) still reckons with the discernment of the opponent. Also, the collection of sayings shows that Jesus in the beginning did not look on the piety of the righteous critically or reject it; think, for example, of the passage of the ninety-nine just who do not need conversion (Lk. 15, 10). So it can be conjectured that at first the authorities of Israel listened to the man from Galilee and did not dispute His proclamation, and that the differences developed clearly only as He began with the inexorability of the prophet to attack the "traditions of the fathers," the theology expounded unanimously by all scholars, and the piety of the leading circles. But the prophetic speech comes only now in its full force and magnitude. That leading class of scholars, judges, and priests represents the people; what is decided there, for good or evil, is binding for the fate of Israel. Even if the individual can choose otherwise for himself, and if the "masses" can remain an object of compassion outside of any decision, the future is decided by the obedience or disobedience of the authorities when faced with the Gospel of God. Thus the prophetic commission demanded of the Prophet a struggle which spared neither the enemy nor Himself.

Within this context there is a series of parables which serve as the prophetic warning and the threatening speech.

1.

Lk. 13, 6-9:

6 And he told this parable: "A man had a fig tree planted in his vineyard; and he came seeking fruit on it and found none. 7And he said to the vinedresser, 'Lo, these three years I have come seeking fruit on this fig tree, and I find none. Cut it down; why should it use up the ground?' 8And he answered him, 'Let it alone, sir, this year also, till I dig about it and put on manure. 9And if it bears fruit next year, well and good; but if not, you can cut it down.' "

Fig trees are planted in the vineyard so that the vines can creep up them.[34] Because of the number and size of its fruit, the

fig tree stands as an archetype of fruitfulness. In this tale it is
not stated clearly whether it is a young or an old tree in question.
If it is an old tree, it would mean the previously fruitful tree
already had no longer borne fruit for three years and thus not
much was to be expected of it anymore. If it is a young sapling, it
had been allowed six years to grown up into a "tree."[35] Now three
more years have passed without its sprouting fruit. In either case,
the decision of the master of the house must seem severe to the
listeners. For fruit trees are tended with great care, and it is ac-
counted a sin to cut one down.[36] Thus a rabbi says: "My son has
died only because he has cut down a fig tree prematurely." The
biblical law protecting trees (Dt. 20, 19) is explained: "The scriptures teach, 'You shall not destroy its trees.' . . . 'You shall eat
from this'—that is a prescription. 'You shall not cut them down'
—that is a prohibition." To fell good trees is reckoned among the
misdeeds which cause "the lights of heaven to darken." So the
pains of the worker to obtain still another delay are understandable.

The threat of the parable becomes clearer if one remembers that
the fruit tree is for the prophets a symbol of Israel, the "plant" of
God. Thus in Psalm 80 the vine becomes a symbol of Israel:
"Thou didst bring a vine out of Egypt; thou didst drive out the
nations and plant it. Thou didst clear the ground for it; it took
deep root and filled the land." (Cf. Ez. 17, 5; 19, 10.) In place
of the vine, as the Letter to the Romans (11, 17) shows, the olive
tree can also be used, and in this case it is the fig tree. Our text
calls to mind the speech of God which Isaiah expounded before
the assembly of the Jewish people, probably in the courtyard of
the temple: "My beloved had a vineyard on a very fertile hill. He
digged it and cleared it of stones, and planted it with choice

vines; . . . and he looked for it to yield grapes, but it yielded wild grapes." This is a metaphor—it is elucidated through the subsequent speech of God: "What more was there to do for my vineyard that I have not done in it? . . . And now I will tell you what I will do to my vineyard. I will remove its hedge, and it shall be devoured; I will break down its wall, and it shall be trampled down. I will make it a waste; it shall not be pruned or hoed, and briers and thorns shall grow up; I will also command the clouds that they rain no rain upon it. For the vineyard of the Lord of hosts is the house of Israel, and the men of Judah are his pleasant planting; . . ." (Is. 5, 4. 5–7).

The parable of Jesus therefore calls up images very familiar to His listeners; it does not need a key. Its application to Israel and the prophetic warning to make use of the respite which has once again been given is perceived clearly.

Luke found this piece in his special matter. Perhaps even there it was already joined to the scene in which Jesus was informed of the misfortune of the Galilean pilgrims who had been killed by Pilate's temple guard as they were making their sacrifice. The answer comes forth in a threat: ". . . Unless you repent you will all likewise perish" (Lk. 13, 3). The parable says the same thing.

2.

The prophetic language, in contrast to the teaching of the scribes, applies to the totality of Israel. So Jesus takes up the language of the prophets and laments "this generation." When a few of the spiritual leaders demand of Him a "sign from heaven" in proof of the truth of His message, He sighs in vexation over the challenge to God and answers, " 'Why does this generation seek a

sign? Truly, I say to you, no sign shall be given to this generation'" (Mk. 8, 12).

"This generation," Jesus says, and "this adulterous and sinful
generation" (Mk. 8, 38). The prophets, too, have spoken thus.
Israel has broken the marriage bond with God (Hos. 2, 2; Is. 57,
3; etc.) and become a whore (Is. 1, 21; Jer. 3, 3; etc.). Like the
prophets, in His contact with the people of His nation Jesus
recognizes that their hearts are closed. Even where this hardness
of heart hides behind the criticism of His public image, His way
of life, and represents itself as pious scandal, He recognizes it. So
He directs His attack at this hypocritical position.

LK. 7, 31–34:
31 To what then shall I compare the men of this generation, and
what are they like?
32 They are like children sitting in the market place and calling
to one another,
"We piped to you,
   and you did not dance;
we wailed,
   and you did not weep."
33 For John the Baptist has come eating no bread and drinking no
wine; and you say, "He has a demon."
34 The Son of man has come eating and drinking; and you say,
"Behold a glutton and a drunkard, a friend of tax collectors and sinners!"

Here we have a discourse which stands in a transitional position between simple comparison and perfected parable. On the
one hand, no story is told; on the other hand, the material compared is presented with great care. It is not merely stated that they
are like peevish children: instead, the kind of children is presented narratively. The one group wishes to play wedding, so
they blow the flutes for a circle dance, but that does not appeal

71

to the others; they wish to play funeral, but that, too, gets no response. It is at these peevish "spoilsports" that the comparison seems to aim; it makes clear what a "perverse generation" is.[37]

Verses 33–35 carry out the comparison and apply it. One might ask whether this is not a compilation. But such a weight lies on this passage that the parable can be understood as an illustration of it: the "perverse generation" is recognized by the indifference with which it rejects Jesus as well as the Baptist, the Baptist on the basis that he is so gloomy with his severe penances that he must be thought a sorcerer, Jesus on the opposite ground that He lacks the severity by which prophets can be recognized. Thus is made clear the ill-will and the hardness which completely destroys the work of the prophetic admonisher.

3.

The parable of the rebellious vinedressers found in three synoptic presentations—Mk. 12, 1–9; Mt. 21, 33–41; Lk. 20, 9–16—displays numerous differences. The linguistic form and the greater or lesser vividness of presentation are not to be touched upon here. But certain differences in the structure should be noted; they could reveal the didactic purpose of the transmitter.

In the following passage we submit a median text from which the peculiarities of the three compositions are comprehensible. It does not in any sense represent the original speech of Jesus, but it exhibits the basic structure which is common to all the versions. Such a text ought not render the synoptic reading superfluous, but on the contrary promote it.

A man planted a vineyard and leased it to vinedressers and left the country.

72

This is the text of Luke, verse 9. In Mark, verse 1, and Matthew, verse 33, we read: ". . . a vineyard, and set a hedge around it, and dug a pit for the wine press, and built a tower." Luke has probably shortened his model; nevertheless, it is possible that the longer text rests upon a subsequent enlargement: the verse which reports the establishment of the vineyard could have recalled the prophetic parable of Is. 5, 1–2, and its beginning could have been installed as an "embellishment."

THE FIRST SENDING OF THE SERVANT

At a given time he sent to the vinedressers a servant, that he might receive his share of the fruit of the vineyard, but they laid hold of him and beat him and sent him away with empty hands.

THE SENDING OF THE SECOND SERVANT

Again he sent a servant to them, but they abused him also and treated him shamefully.

So far, the versions agree in essentials. But then Mark, and Luke following him, speaks of a third sending. Mark, verse 5: "And he sent another, and him they killed." Luke, verse 12: "And he sent yet a third; this one they wounded and cast out." The sending of a third servant does not occur in Matthew; there it is already the son who is sent in the third place. In this way it corresponds to the theme of the three steps which is used so often. Mark and Luke have probably enlarged their versions in order to maintain a three-count in the sending of the servants. They arrange the story so that the son does not merely stand in the row of messengers, but is contrasted with the balanced group of servants.

Finally he sent his son to them, for he thought: they will have respect for my son.

This is the statement of Matthew, verse 37. Luke, verse 13, says: "I will send my beloved son." Mark, with strong emphasis, says: "He had still one other, a beloved son; finally he sent him to them."

But the vinedressers said to one another: This one is the heir; let us kill him, and then the inheritance will be ours. And they laid hold of him and killed him and threw him out of the vineyard.

This is what we find in Mark, verse 8. But Matthew, verse 39, and Luke, verse 15, put it in reversed order: "They cast him out of the vineyard and killed him."

Now what will the lord of the vineyard do? He will come and annihilate the vinedressers.

All the versions conclude with the idea that the vineyard would be given over to others. Matthew even says expressly (v. 41): "He will . . . let out the vineyard to other tenants who will give him the fruits in their seasons."

First of all, the story as such must be considered. Anyone laying out a new vineyard is taking a great deal of trouble and risk upon himself; that is true just as much for the time of Jesus as for the time of Isaiah, and it is true even today. The ground chosen must be freed from weeds and stones. In the mountains it must be terraced. To guard against animals it must be encircled with a bramble hedge or with a wall. Since grapes deteriorate by overripening, a winepress must be built; the grapes are trod in the upper vat, and the must can collect in the lower. Because a watchman must live in the vineyard from the beginning of the ripening season, and because it is customary that his entire family lodge there at the time of harvest, a hut is built out of branches, or a stone substructure is erected upon which the hut is built.[38] Considering the trouble and care involved, the reader not only understands the phrase "costly vineyard," but also sees that the garden which makes for its possessor so much work and care represents in the prophetic discourse a symbol for Israel, the "planting of God." Thus it comes about that already in the first sentence of the tale, whether or not he recalls the parable of Isaiah, the listener understands that the discourse concerns an affair between God and Israel.

The story continues with the owner of the vineyard going out of the land and, when he could expect the young vine shoots to have reached bearing age, sending his servant back to collect the rent in the form of produce. Even this detail is not pure invention; it is sufficiently verified that even before the time of the Gospel large parts of the Galilean highlands were in the hands of foreign landlords.[39] A papyrus, for example, attests that a finance minister of the Ptolemaic Empire in the third century before Christ owned a piece of property in Galilee which supplied him with his wine in Egypt. The story says nothing beyond this.[40] But further aspects can be imagined: the farmers are hostile; indeed, in the Galilean area there were zealots burning to reestablish the freedom of Israel. The farmers therefore refuse the demand for rent and drive the messengers of the lord away, and when he finally sends his son and heir, who, unlike the servants, represents his person, then they do not submit, but instead take the opportunity to bring the land into their own possession again. When the heir is done away with, only the death of the lord must still be awaited, for according to Jewish law the possessions of a person dying without an heir were ownerless goods, and such property belonged to the first person who seized possession of it.[41] This fact shows that the proceedings described could be plausible to the hearers, and with this the stipulation of credibility is fulfilled, so that we may speak of a genuine parable.

But it is further demanded of a parable not only that the story be imaginable and understandable, but that the logic of its sequence and dynamic of its crucial point make an insight inevitable. That, too, is true here. The owner has had no success with his servants, so he finally sends his son because he expects that the son will be respected as he himself would be. And with the sending of the son the events are drawn to the decisive point: he is killed and dishonored. But for this, there is only one answer, an answer which is clear to every hearer: the annihilating judgment.

The concentration on the turning point makes everything else in the story of the parable preliminary. This also can be seen here. The figure of the foreign lord is unsympathetic throughout to the hearers, but this comes not from the lord himself but from his conduct at the decisive place in the plot. That the lord demands only his portion of the produce of the harvest is likewise stipulated by the construction of the story. If it were a purely hypothetical tale, it could be simpler and more informative; then perhaps a native householder who wished to go on a trip would have confided the vineyard to his own servants, and what he would have demanded would have been the entire harvest profit.

Like the other parables already observed, and to an even greater degree, this story employs typical figures. So it happens that the entire plot, meaningful in itself, is accompanied by a connected course of events also meaningful in itself but lying on a higher plane. This must now be examined more carefully.

Such a figure is the man who has laid out the vineyard and demands his share of the profit. It points to God, as elsewhere the figure of the lord of the house, or the shepherd, or the king, does. It is expected of the hearers, who are accustomed to parables, that they recognize in the conduct of the foreign lord God's way of acting. Their sympathy may in the beginning be on the side of the vinedressers, but the development of the story makes that quickly forgotten. The brutality of the vinedressers which increases even to murder, and on the other side the forbearing patience of the lord and his moving goodness which leads him to place his son in danger in the firm expectation that all would now resolve itself peacefully, forces them to agree when, in the end, judgment is spoken of.

This one figure alone would suffice to reveal the meaning of the parable. But there are still others. If the servants of the lord are his messengers, and in his name lay claim to the profit from his planting, then they point to the prophets who as "servants of God" indeed had had the commission to demand God's rights of Israel.

But then the figure of the son is also meaningful on the higher level. He comes as the last after the line of prophets and is so much more than they that there is hope his errand will succeed. He represents God in a much higher way than the prophets, and therefore the atrocity to him necessarily draws the judgment down upon itself. The figure with its fate which stands in focus, in which not only the narrative of the lower plane but also the course of events on the higher level have their pivot, can only be the Messiah. But this assertion demands a series of further explanations.

The fact that in the Jewish writings handed down the Messiah is nowhere called the "Son" of God causes a certain difficulty. But it must be borne in mind that the synoptic tradition presumes this Messiah title as recognized and acknowledged, and furthermore that the title has an Old Testament origin—one thinks, for example, of the words of promise to the descendants of David: "I will be his father, and he shall be my son" (2 Sam. 7, 14), and the adoption speech in the messianically understood second psalm: "You are my son, today I have begotten you" (Ps. 2, 7). What the silence of the Jewish witnesses indicates, and thus the problem we have to reckon with, is that in the Hellenistic time a sharp repulse of Gentile notions was necessary, and therefore everything which might bring to mind gods and sons of gods, even within Jewish thought itself, was to be shunned.[42] But this appears not to hold true for the time, and above all not for the particular surroundings of Jesus; there the Messiah, on account of His relation to God as the called and anointed of God, as His trusted and beloved, could be called the Son of God.

If this passage is now taken to be a speech of Jesus, then it doubtlessly reveals a messianic claim. Jesus is saying nothing less than that the demand which God has made of Israel is raised and represented through Him differently than it ever was through the prophets, and further that because of this His work, He is in danger of being killed; He is saying that this killing of one sent by God, should it come to that, will for that very reason—because it is not the killing of a prophet but the killing of the Messiah—deliver Israel up to the judgment of God. What is said here is such a revelation of the situation in which the responsible ones of the people find themselves and, forced by the gravity of conditions, such a clear stand by Jesus, that concealment in parable form is understandable.

Here now exegesis must take a position and make a decision. If it goes beyond a mere rendering of the text, which of course is inevitable with historical methods, and ventures a critique on the matter, then it will not admit the idea that God has appointed a man to the office of the One upon whom salvation depends— the Messiah. It will be inclined to suppose that the community of disciples, moved by subjective experiences and enticed by mythological archetypes present in the Jewish expectations, has elevated the figure of the holy teacher and raised it above the mass of men. But then it would be necessary to consider a speech revealing such a pretension also a production of the "community." If, beyond that, exegesis is convinced that Jesus has spoken only pure parables—which incidentally is confirmed so far—but that the community had not understood them sufficiently to improve them, perhaps because its preaching could not restrain itself as much as is necessary for the shaping of a pure parable, then it will have an inclination, even a tendency, to demonstrate the passages as allegory.

But the opposite line of reasoning can also work. Then the deliberation goes like this: we are dealing with a genuine parable, and there is no solid reason to understand it as fabricated allegory. The reference added in the final movement of the story to the dialogue of the transaction between God and His people demonstrates Jesus' conviction that the history of Israel has now approached closer to catastrophe, indeed has already entered into the critical phase. It is shown further that even Jesus thought of Himself as commissioned by God, for which reason the resistance of Israel to God comes to a head; and further, that just as the situation which originated with His appearance differentiated itself through the urgent nearness of the future event from all times which went before, so also His commission and His position in God's work distinguish Him from all that was to be found in the prophets. He understands Himself as the last one whom God sends to His people, and in obedience to the decree of God He must conceive of Himself as the highest who would ever be sent —in the language of the prophetic tradition, as the Messiah. The claim of Jesus is distinct, but at the same time disguised. To call Himself the Messiah is not His business, but that of those who have recognized Him and His work and His commission.

Thus the two positions are to be balanced against one another. Here, where not confessions but the exegesis of texts is being treated, we are concerned not with the question which of the two better corresponds to the faith of the Church, but which is correct for the text under discussion.

4.

That such a speech of Jesus was of highest significance for the early Christian preaching is obvious. So the reader should not be surprised that we scrutinize the story of the parable carefully.

Probably the quotation from Isaiah—the reminiscence of that famous image in which God himself raises a lament over the planting which he laid out so lovingly and which had proved fruitless—already presents an amplification of the original wording. The tale loses in suspense thereby; its point is, so to speak, divulged too early. But that does not correspond to Jesus' teaching method, which can be recognized in many places. He draws the story tautly and directly to its climax, and heightens the perception arising there by the moment of surprise. The writer Luke has suppressed the quotation which he read in Mark, possibly out of just such considerations.

The number three in any case plays a role in the structure of the tale. But the three steps, which in order to conform with the sending of two servants put the son in third place—as in Matthew —may correspond to the older tradition.[43] Mark's composition, which Luke is perhaps following, gives rise to the impression that the sending of a third servant was developed out of the material of the first two. Such expansion could happen in order to link together the efficacy of the prophets of the old era through the number three and to contrast to it the work of the Messiah as an act of a completely new kind.

Mark's version also plainly shows the strongest emphasis on the figure of the son. In Matthew, the unaccentuated speech of the story tells that the owner sent "his son"; Luke speaks of the "beloved son," which means primarily just "the one who is heir." Mark goes further and states with emphasis that the lord had only this one son whom he could send, and had sent him as the "*eschatos*," in God's intention the "last"; while Matthew produces the expression, fitting to the story, of "*hysteron*," which in an adverbial form is equivalent to "later," or "finally," and then without emphasis designates the end of a series.

On the other hand, in Matthew and Luke there is a significant alteration of Mark's pattern where it is said that the tenants kill the son and disfigure his dead body by abandoning it to the wild animals. With striking accord, Matthew and Luke have here turned the text around: the son is first thrown out of the vineyard, and then he is killed outside. Obviously, the interests of the preaching rule here. It takes the parable as prophecy and wishes to find the messianic fate of Jesus announced in it as precisely as possible. For this purpose, the circumstance that Jesus was killed outside the holy city was highly significant. So the easily altered wording of the parable reflects what is preached in the Letter to the Hebrews: "For the bodies of those animals whose blood is brought into the sanctuary by the high priest as a sacrifice for sin are burned outside the camp. So Jesus also suffered outside the gate in order to sanctify the people through his own blood. Therefore let us go forth to him outside the camp, bearing abuse for him" (13, 11-13).

The elucidations in the parable itself are trifling, and its thrust appears undeflectible. Nevertheless, the proclamation stands out strongly at the end.

Perhaps the last sentence of the parable already is expanded. When the murderers are annihilated, the event indeed comes to its conclusion. To add that the vineyard is given to other tenants does not seem to fit the tautness of Jesus' speech. The intention of this rounding off is shown in the writing of Matthew. Here it is said first of all with a certain breadth: "He will . . . let out the vineyard to other tenants who will give him the fruits in their seasons." Then the theme is taken up again later, and it is now expressly declared: "Therefore I tell you, the kingdom of God will be taken away from you and given to a nation producing the fruits of it" (Mt. 21, 43). Contained within is the thought presented in the threatening speech of Jesus that the Gentiles shall walk in Israel's place; here, too, the proclaimers in no way "produce," but only draw out what is explicitly stated in other places, as, for example, in the passage: "I tell you, many will come from east and west and sit at table with Abraham, Isaac, and Jacob in the kingdom of heaven, while the sons of the kingdom will be thrown into the outer darkness; there men will weep and gnash their teeth" (Mt. 8, 11f.; cf. Lk. 13, 28-30).

But perhaps more important to the proclamation than the idea of the Gentiles is the theme of the Messiah. It is present in the parable, but reference is made only to the dangerous, catastrophic possibility that even the last messenger of God, the Messiah, will be slain. Therefore, the proclaimers see themselves forced to use means to carry out the theme of the messianic way to the very end.

The image of the rejection and choosing of the stone found in Psalm 118 is already in Jewish interpretation referred to such leader figures as Abraham and King David, and so also to the Messiah.[44] The Christian proclamation has evidently admitted it as a prophetic announcement of the fate of Jesus, as one of the passages which speak of His rejection by Israel and His exaltation by God. So we find in one of the Petrine texts (Acts 4, 10–12): ". . . be it known to you all, and to all people of Israel, that by the name of Jesus Christ of Nazareth, whom you crucified, whom God raised from the dead, by him this man is standing before you well. This is the stone which was rejected by you builders, but which has become the head of the corner. And there is salvation in no one else . . . ," and in the First Letter of Peter (2, 4. 6): "Come to him, to that living stone, rejected by men but in God's sight chosen and precious; . . . For it stands in scripture: 'Behold, I am laying in Zion a stone, a cornerstone chosen and precious, and he who believes in him will not be put to shame.' To you therefore who believe, he is precious, but for those who do not believe, 'The very stone which the builders rejected has become the head of the corner,' and 'A stone that will make men stumble, a rock that will make them fall. . . .'" So it now seems pertinent to cite this psalm text in order to draw the theme of the messianic fate to an end. Mark annexes it simply and unobtrusively through the expression: "Have you not read this scripture . . . ?" Luke reports first of all of the reaction to the parable. The listeners are shaken by the threat and shout: "God forbid!"; then they look at Jesus to discover what can explain His seriousness and what He now has to say to them, and then with the text of the psalm He batters their terrified defense.

This passage speaks of the stone which the workmen disdained and rejected but which God made the base and the crown of His building.[45] So the completion of the messianic way, which was not to be found in the parable, is highlighted, and we have here a demonstration of how Christian proclamation uses the parables.

5.

In Matthew, the parable of the great banquet follows that of the vinedressers. The order of that series will be preserved here, because the first parable clarifies many details in Matthew's version of the second. The version offered by Luke is considerably different from that of the Gospel of Matthew. Both have probably borrowed from different written sources and present the result of a longer process of tradition. When, therefore, we speak of the mode of action of "Matthew" or of "Luke," we mean the influences which were in part already at work before the evangelists.

Mт. 22, 2–10	Lк. 14, 16–24
2 The kingdom of heaven may be compared to a king who gave a marriage feast for his son,	16 A man once gave a great banquet, and invited many;
3 and sent his servants to call those who were invited to the marriage feast; but they would not come.	17 and at the time for the banquet he sent his servant to say to those who had been invited, "Come; for all is now ready."

4 Again he sent other servants, saying, "Tell those who are invited, Behold, I may have made ready my dinner, my oxen and my fat calves are killed, and everything is ready; come to the marriage feast."

5 But they made light of it and went off, one to his farm another to his business,

18 But they all alike began to make excuses. The first said to him, "I have bought a field, and I must go out and see it; I pray you, have me excused." ¹⁹And another said, "I have bought five yoke of oxen, and I go to examine them; I pray you, have me excused." ²⁰And another said, "I have married a wife, and therefore I cannot come."

6 while the rest seized his servants, treated them shamefully, and killed them.

21 So the servant came and reported this to his master.

7 The king was angry, and he sent his troops and destroyed those murderers and burned their city.

Then the householder in anger

8 Then he said to his servants, "The wedding is ready, but those invited were not worthy.

said to his servant, "Go out quickly to the streets and lanes of the city, and bring in the poor and maimed and blind and lame." ²²And the servant said, "Sir, what you commanded has been done, and still there is room." ²³And the master said to the servant, "Go out to the high-

9 Go therefore to the thoroughfares, and invite to the mar-

ways and hedges, and compel

riage feast as many as you find."

10 And those servants went out into the streets and gathered all whom they found, both bad and good; so the wedding hall was filled with guests.

people to come in, that my house may be filled.

24 For I tell you, none of those men who were invited shall taste my banquet."

What is essential in the incident told in both versions can be reproduced in three sentences: A well-to-do man summons his fellow citizens to a festive banquet. Those invited decline amid excuses. The offended man thereupon fetches the poor to his table in their stead.

The people who were invited are distinguished and well-to-do. Anyone who can buy five yoke of oxen to add to his beasts of burden—property is measured by the "oxen-power" needed to plough it; a small farmer possesses land for only one or two yoke of oxen—is a man of property. The other guests are to be evaluated similarly. In sharp contrast to them stand the cripples, the blind, and the lame, who comprise "the poor," for they are incapable of working and are therefore referred to as beggars. Alongside them stand the people outside by the highways and garden walls; they are the homeless. Upon this contrast of rich and honored and poor, despised people the tale depends. The rather improbable detail that those invited first of all decline, and the exasperated host then fetches the very poorest into his house, is conceivable—and that is sufficient for a parable—if one draws in for comparison another story, which supposes a real occurrence. It is reported of a tax collector, Bar Ma'Jan: "Once he prepared a breakfast for the town councillors, but they did not come. Then he said: The poor shall come and eat it up, that it is not wasted." A tax collector was not "socially acceptable"; so one can imagine that, after he had become rich, he had attempted to enter the "better circles" among his fellow citizens but was repulsed by them.[46] So it may be that Jesus' listeners immediately see through the excuses of those invited immediately as pretexts and, understanding the mortification of the master of the house so much the more strongly, grasp what is expressly said: that he flew into a passion and in his indignation had his house filled with the poor.

No key is included for the parable, but the allusion to the "great banquet" already awakes attention immediately. The festive banquet amid the patriarchally composed family and the circle of friends, a cultural form taken over from earlier times, furnishes in the discourses of Jesus as in late Jewish scriptures an image of the blessed company in the completed time of salvation.[47] Thus the gaze of the hearer is directed to the future, and the central theme of Jesus' discourse is again in the present. If one considers the plan of the tale from this point, the invitation to the banquet becomes clear immediately; it refers to the call of the Gospel. But with this the course of events also becomes clear: the exasperated master of the house declares that those invited first are not worthy of the dinner (Mt., v. 8; Lk., v. 24). He directs that another new invitation go forth, and there begins the odd picture of a dinner at which the master has the poor, distressed, and homeless as table companions.

The parable obviously supports the prophetic warning speech. But it must be asked who is addressed. Undoubtedly, the passage is directed at the responsible leaders of Israel; but it remains an open question whether the one group of men from whom salvation is diverted and the other to whom it falls are seen *within* Israel, in which case it would be the circle of the Pharisaical scripture scholars and its followers who are examined and the people disdained by them—in Pharisaical usage the "uneducated" and the "sinners"—who are contrasted to them; or whether, on the other hand, it is Israel as a whole, represented by its authorities, to which the despised mass of Gentiles is contrasted. This question will now be pursued.

The first thing to be considered is what weight the proclamation of Jesus laid upon the threat to Israel and the idea that salvation could be withdrawn from the people of the covenant and pass over to the Gentiles. This is an extension of a theme which appears already in the prophets. The summoning of the Gentiles to participate in the grace of Israel is first of all a theme of promise (cf., for example, Is. 45, 6; 49, 12; 59, 19; Jer. 3, 18). But the other side is also already visible: Israel is aroused by the threat that the Gentiles might not merely be summoned to salvation alongside and with it, so that Mount Zion would become the center of the world (cf. Is. 2, 2-6), but instead be called in its place and on the basis of its rejection—Malachi's speech of God comes to mind: "I have no pleasure in you, says the Lord of hosts, and I will not accept an offering from your hand. For from the rising of the sun to its setting my name is great among the nations, and in every place incense is offered to my name, and a pure offering; for my name is great among the nations . . ." (Mal. 1, 10ff.). Along this line lie the prophetic threatening words of Jesus that the many will come from the ends of the earth and gather at the eschatological banquet with the patriarchs of Israel; but those who have called themselves the "sons of the kingdom" are seen as cast into the darkness outside (Mt. 8, 11f. = Lk. 13, 28).

Matthew appears to have preserved this comprehensive meaning of the parable. Even the context in which he transmits the composition shows this. It stands in the series of encounters which follow upon the procession into Jerusalem in chapters 21–25 and in particular in the portion 21, 1—24, 3. Although there are also pieces there which focus upon the authorities within Israel (21, 18–32; 22, 23–33. 34–40; 23, 1–36), the stress does lie on that aspect in which the messianic position and fullness of power of Jesus stands out (21, 10–17. 23–27; 22, 15–22. 41–46), and, corresponding closely to the majestic title of the "anointed," the fate of the totality of Israel (21, 18f. 20–22. 33–46—here, in 22, 1–14, there follows the parable of the banquet—and 23, 37—24, 3).

The construction of the parable in Matthew's version, then, also shows in its basic contents a clear twofold division. There is only the group of the first-invited on the one side, and that of those coming in their place on the other side. The second group comes from the streets which lead as "exits" beyond the city boundary out into foreign lands, and the walls of the gardens which lie outside. Both expressions exist, of course, only within the scope of the story, and describe the homeless people only in contrast to the respected citizens. But Matthew, as further observations will show, apparently understood them as references to the Gentiles.

If one acknowledges the division as part of the original form and sees the parable in the service of the prophetic threatening, then it is to be accepted as highly probable that Jesus' discourse was indeed directed at the authorities of Israel, but in such a way that in it Israel itself was addressed. The judgment is placed before the eyes of the people who see salvation guaranteed by the covenant of Sinai. God can, despite the covenant, take salvation from Israel and give it to others. And the decision rests upon the message of God which Jesus proclaims.

The parable thus falls within the general scope of Jesus' encounter with Israel. It not merely serves as a scholarly elucidation of the prophetic message, but it bears and executes it. In it there occurs a merciless assault on the fundamental consciousness of vocation of Israel. The speech sounds different from any other instruction given to the people. It leads to a decision: either it is recognized as the word that God speaks to Israel on the basis of the covenant, which it supplants, or it is refused as a heretical usurpation and leads to the annihilation of Jesus.

The preaching of the apostles shows how the theme of Israel and the Gentiles has remained decisive in the early church. So one may suppose that just as Paul, for example in chapters 9–11 of the Letter to the Romans, used his reflection to disclose to the Gentile Christians the secret of their amnesty, that they might acknowledge it humbly, so too in their own way the communities of Matthew deliberated upon the fate of Israel and the vocation of the Gentiles. With such an explanation the parable maintains its meaning as an expression of a threat which has essentially come to pass.

Of course, the composition which the tradition appearing in Luke's version has given to the parable is also comprehensible if one proceeds from the interests of the early Christian preaching. To be fair, it must be noted that the contrast between the first-invited Israel and the Gentiles brought in in its place has a genuine correspondence in a contrast within Israel. Such a contrast does indeed exist between the group of the "just" who imagine themselves accepted by God for their fulfillment of the law, and the "sinners," who according to the judgment of the first group have lost the favor of God for a long time or forever. That such a contrast also plays a meaningful role in the encounter of Jesus with the authorities can be seen in one example among many in the words of the Lord, beginning with the solemnly assuring "Truly I say to you": "the tax collectors and the harlots go into the kingdom of God before you"—that means "instead of you" (Mt. 21, 31).[48]

The theme of the merciful calling, of its rejection and the turning of salvation to those who seem not to be called, is therefore also valid in a kind of limited way within Israel, and in this form it is enlightening for the decision of the individual for his faith, his image of God, his understanding of salvation. And it is on this theme that Luke has collected the proclamatory materials of interest. Just as he brings out of his own special matter those reports which show and teach how a lost one is brought home to God—the sinner in the house of the Pharisee (Lk. 7, 36), the head tax collector Zacchaeus (Lk. 19, 1), and, in the parables, the tax collector in the temple (18, 9) and the lost son (15, 11)—so also the parable of the banquet, without turning its attention away from the Gentiles, speaks to him in the first place of the calling of the sinners in place of the "just." That Luke himself wishes to accentuate it in this way is proved by the textual context in which he has placed the parable. It is found in a group of events and discourses which are inserted within the framework of a Sabbath dinner in the house of a Pharisaic chief (14, 1–24) and forms there a definite answer to the exclamation of one of the table companions: "Blessed is he who shall eat bread in the kingdom of God!" (v. 15). The parable seems to contrast the danger of this attitude with the phrase which appears to have been spoken with the same unsuspecting confidence as had earlier been revealed in the selection of the places of honor (vv. 7–11). The Pharisee at the table had called himself blessed; the parable, on the other hand, ends with the sentence: "For I tell you, none of those men who were invited shall taste my banquet."

* * *

Luke's version of the parable can be evaluated according to this preliminary consideration. The action narrated stands in two acts; the invitation of the fellow citizens and their refusals form the first, the invitation of the poor the second. The version of Luke—unlike that of Matthew—presents the first in a manner of a vivid storyteller, but is nevertheless clear and direct in its course. The second act begins just as clearly with the statement that the lord becomes angry at the servant's report (v. 21). But in the presentation of the second act Matthew appears to have preserved the original simplicity and Luke to have enlarged the basic text. What was originally a calling of the poor is now explained in two distinguishable calls. The second of these (v. 23) corresponds exactly to the one which Matthew (vv. 9–10) reports, and it, too, has the Gentiles in mind. The first, on the other hand, Luke seems to have fashioned new. One sees how he proceeds. When the setting presents the world of the Gentiles outside on the highway, the city becomes meaningful in contrast to it. "The city" is plainly Jerusalem, and Jerusalem is the symbol of Israel. Now it is said that even in the "city," within Israel itself, there are the poor, and that these are fetched in the place of the rich and respected as the first at the banquet—the words of the Lord reported shortly before seem to be echoed in the demand that one should summon the poor instead of the rich to dinner (14, 13). If, however, it is clear that the basic text, when it speaks of respected and wretched, has in mind a spiritual contrast, that between the original hearers of the call and those fetched in their place, then it is also to be assumed of the expansion that the poor of which it speaks are to be conceived of in a spiritual sense. It is the sinners, therefore, who are thought of, and the contrast is made within Israel between those who as the "just" think their call is secure and those who seem to the superficial glance to be the lost.

So there are in Luke's version within the frame of the one parable two very differently constructed contrasts: 1) the just and the sinners within Israel, and 2) Israel and the Gentiles; the two are mingled together, and here already it is clear that Luke's amplification is secondary. Nevertheless, the assertion must be evaluated. The theme of the calling of the Gentiles could and evidently should not be suppressed, but that of the calling of sinners was the proclamation which Luke urgently advocated. The contrast between the just man who feels his acceptance by God secure—just as it was described earlier in the parable-like passage on the place of honor at the banquet—and the man who in the knowledge of the holiness of God and of his own sin discovers the truth and finds the attitude which alone corresponds to it (cf. Lk. 18, 9), is a great theme of the salvific proclamation. Perhaps it is characteristic of the area of the Church in which the Gospel of Luke had to work that the question of the calling of Israel and the calling of the Gentiles had retreated into the background in favor of the question of the true and false relationship to God, and just as characteristic for the area in which the

93

Gospel of Matthew worked that the call had remained in the foreground.

* * *

With this, the attention turns to the peculiarities of Matthew's version; they show up, as already indicated, in the first section of the tale. The host is here a king. To tell it in this manner is obviously for the benefit of the Jewish-Christian realm; parables about kings are copiously represented in the rabbinical tradition. The dinner to which the king sends invitations is described as the wedding feast which he prepares for his son. But because the figure of the son plays no role in the further development of the story, the intention of the evangelist is already recognizable here. The banquet of the original tale is at its consummation to be elucidated as the dinner of the eschatological consummation in the midst of which stands the glorified Messiah. From this follows a second important peculiarity. The host sends his message twice to the same guests. We are not dealing here with the preliminary invitation customary in the Orient and then the final fetching of the invited guests after the conclusion of the preparations, but rather with a renewed attempt to win the same people, for it is expressly said that they decline the first invitation: "they would not come" (v. 3). The summons to dinner is therefore stated more urgently; a request is included when the king directs the servant to say: "Behold, I have made ready my dinner, my oxen and my fat calves are killed, and everything is ready; come to the marriage feast" (v. 4). But the refusal, too, now becomes sharper. According to Luke, those summoned at least preserve appearances; they produce—and this in genuine narrative fashion is shown in three examples—excuses, polite subterfuges which

94

disguise their no. Matthew has only terse phrases for this, but he speaks expressly of the disdain with which the invitation is handled: "But they made light of it and went off, one to his farm, another to his business" (v. 5). Then he intensifies it once again as he adds: "while the rest seized his servants, treated them shamefully, and killed them" (v. 6). Accordingly, the reaction of the insulted king is now also of the most extreme severity. The phrase in the basic text, "The king was angry," which introduces the second act, the fetching of the poor (Lk., v. 21), is now projected into a forceful conclusion for the first act (Mt., v. 7). The king in his anger sends out an army against the rebels. They are now no longer "fellow citizens," but, corresponding to the elevation of the master of the house to king, mighty vassals who possess a fortified city. The army lays siege to the city, overcomes it and burns it, and its lords are killed.

Naturally, such expressive intensifications distort the tale; the logic of its course is disturbed, absurdity arises from the fact that the wedding banquet still stands prepared after the military expedition which even includes the siege and storming of the city. But the difficulty is removed as soon as we reflect that the plane of the "story drawn from life" is, at least at this point, already abandoned, and a higher meaning, that of the spiritual, has entered the action. The genuine parable moves with clear intent on the lower plane and proves itself by creating an entrance to a higher truth; the discourse of the criminal court of the king does the opposite: in it the higher meaning penetrates the matter of the tale and makes it run rampant; it uses such heavy accents that the treatment reaches a conclusion already at this point, and what follows is degraded to a "supplement." Here there can be discovered an activity of the proclamation which

95

was already recognizable several times earlier. But in these the substance of the parable was not disturbed. The application of its subject matter to another assertion—in other words, its allegorization—was effected through subsequent additions. For examples one might take the supplementary statements of the parable of the vinedressers (Mt. 21, 42f.) and the text which was added in the literary composition of the parable of the wedding (Mk. 2, 18ff.), and remember the allegorizing explanations of the parable of the sowing (Mk. 4, 14ff.) and of the parable of the weeds (Mt. 13, 24ff.): they all held themselves at a distance from the parable. Here now, for the first time, it can be seen how a proclamation which extends out beyond the intention of the parable penetrates into the parable itself and changes its wording.

It was observed earlier that the proclaimers had no tendency, and obviously did not consider themselves authorized, to make such interpretations with their own words. It could be said that they do not "produce," but "apply"; everything that they say has its basis and at least its support in the tradition proceeding from Jesus. So now it must also be asked where Matthew has found the material with which he is able to extend and round out the first scene of the action so forcefully.

The parable of the banquet stands in Matthew's version in intimate association with that of the vinedressers. The conversation partners are the same ones whom Jesus had opposed already after the purification of the temple (21, 23), the same who were expressly addressed in the concluding comments to the parable of the vinedressers (21, 42-46), and to whom the parable of the banquet is now told (22, 1). The scene, therefore, remains the same, and the two discourses complete one another.

The meaning of the parable of the vinedressers was given at

the end in a postscript: "The kingdom of God will be taken away from you and given to a nation producing the fruits of it." This corresponds to the change made when the man who organized the banquet is presented as a king and when the fellow citizens of the master of the house appear as mighty vassals and their offensive indifference in the face of the invitation is heightened to an act of rebellion. The figure of the son, who stood at the pivot of the parable of the vinedressers, also continues in the picture, and so the banquet becomes a wedding feast for the king's son. The close connection of the parables now leads—and this is worth noticing—to a transfer of subject matter; the description of the conflict as well as the act of punishment is now developed in conformity with the model of the first parable.[49] Where the parable of the vinedressers said, "He sent his servants to the tenants, to get his fruit" (21, 34), the second states that he "sent his servants to call those who were invited to the marriage feast" (22, 3); where the first said, "Again he sent other servants" (21, 36), this says the same word for word. Where in the first the misdeed of the vinedressers was described, "The tenants took his servants and beat one, killed another, and stoned another" (21, 35), this states, "The rest seized his servants, treated them shamefully, and killed them." From the parable of the vinedressers, therefore, comes the repeated invitation and the refusal which grows to brutal violence. But the presentation of the punishment also stems from the parable of the vinedressers, for there it forms the conclusion and climax and bears the prophetic threat in the judgment: "When therefore the owner of the vineyard comes, what will he do to those tenants? . . . He will put those wretches to a miserable death" (21, 41). And just as there the verse was completed with the confirmation that the lord will give his vineyard to "others," here, in the second scene of the story, the calling of the "others" is described.

After these individual observations Matthew's version can now be examined as a whole. The two invitations in the first scene, which differ neither in content nor in the persons addressed, evidently present the repeated and more and more urgent call to Israel through the prophetic message. The message is declined, and the messengers are mishandled and killed. With the punishment this theme comes to an end. It seems likely that the destruction of Jerusalem, that judgment upon Israel which seemed to the early Christian proclamation to be a significant prefiguring of the Last Judgment (cf. Mt. 24), here determines the presentation. If that is true, Matthew settles the consideration of the fate of Israel in this passage. But then his attention wanders to the others, the Gentiles who have been fetched into the house of the king in Israel's place, to those of the peoples who have heard the inviting call of the Gospel and followed it. If that means that the wedding hall is full of guests, then the passage seems to lack little of an express statement that this band of those called into the house of the king portrays the community of disciples, the Church. In conclusion, we must note one peculiarity of Matthew's version which falls outside the framework. After the conclusion, which was reached with the confirmation "the wedding hall was filled with guests," the story begins again and now develops a new and different scene.

Mt. 22, 11–14:

11 But when the king came in to look at the guests, he saw there a man who had no wedding garment; [12]and he said to him, "Friend, how did you get in here without a wedding garment?" And he was speechless. [13]Then the king said to the attendants, "Bind him hand

98

and foot, and cast him into the outer darkness; there men will weep and gnash their teeth." [14]For many are called, but few are chosen.

What is related here is not only set off from the main text of the parable formally, but also does not agree properly in content. It was said before that the poor should be fetched from the streets; but how then can it be demanded that they appear in wedding garments?

An attempted answer has been made with the explanation that the guests of such invitations are given wedding garments, and the man had simply refused to put his on. Such information is presumed and has no support in the text.[50]

A more enlightening conjecture is that Matthew has here added on what was originally an independent "Parable of the Wedding Garment" in order to make a further assertion. To be sure, one should not then speak of a parable, but of a parable-fragment, for it lacks a preliminary story which would lead up to the decisive incident and make it understandable.[51] How such a parable must have looked when complete can perhaps be shown in an example. It is reported of a rabbi of the first century after Christ, Jochanan ben Zakkai, that he said: "It is like a king who invited his servants to a banquet. But he did not stipulate the time to them. The wise among them dressed themselves and went down to the entrance of the palace. . . . But the foolish went about their work; they said to themselves: Can there then be a banquet without laborious preparation? Suddenly the king desired his guests. The wise went before him as they were, dressed, and the foolish as they were, soiled. The king rejoiced over the wise and was angry with the foolish. He said: These who have dressed themselves for the dinner shall sit and eat and drink, but those who have not dressed for dinner shall stand and look on."[52]

Here the decisive act has a preliminary story which makes it plausible. The earlier "Parable of the Wedding Garment" may have been similar. The guest, then—like the bridesmaids who had taken no provision of oil along—would be convicted of foolish levity or lack of regard for the majesty of the king.

It can be imagined that it did not suit the proclaimers to preserve the entire parable, and therefore they present two instead of the one encompassing parable. If the preliminaries are broken away, then the subordinating bond to the main parable is made clear. But then the second section of the main parable must be made into a preliminary story, and that is evidently what happened. In one interpolation, which clearly departs from the parable level, it is said of the poor that there are among them "both bad and good." In this way the attention is redirected to the introductory sentence in verse 8. It is thus not sufficient to have received and accepted the grace of the call and to proceed into the house of the king; rather, man's worthiness is even then still demanded; the guest must act in such a way that the king can suffer him at the table. Here the fragment begins, and the new action starts. The king enters to visit his guests; then he walks to one who apparently has not understood what it means to partake of the table of the king and attend the wedding of his son. With the same severity which had annihilated the rebels, the disrespectful guest is laid in chains and thrown into the darkness.

It is again shown that the sequence which in more than one place appears clumsy and absurd on the level of pure parable is clear as soon as it is considered on the level of spiritual meaning, as an allegorical passage. The earlier question, for example, of how it could be demanded of the poor man that he possess a wedding garment, resolves itself on this level; for here the garment is nothing but the expression of an inner disposition. A rabbinical passage can show how the term is used: "If the scriptures [simply] spoke of white clothes, how many white garments have not the peoples of the world! But see, it speaks of fulfillment of the commandments and good works and study of the laws" (Rabbi Jochanan ben Zakkai). Another one demands that a man spend his entire life in penance in order to be arrayed for death, using the scriptural basis, "At every time let thy clothes be white!" (Rabbi Eliezer).[53]

So the early Christian preaching, which relies upon the original parable but at the same time cites other traditional matter, and which is led in everything by the insight which the Holy Ghost gives into God's grace, stands out clearly. With the judgment of destruction and annihilation the story of the old people of the covenant was provisionally closed. In its place another "people" has now stepped (21, 43), called together from the peoples of the world by the Gospel (28, 19f.). But the sermon is not yet concluded. It permits the threat of the original parable to remain and holds it warningly before the community of the disciples, who, of course, not by merit, but by a merciful call, are in the embrace of God's salvation. But they are not yet beyond the Last Judgment; they must still pass through that trial whose authority to separate will reach into their midst. The words of the Lord will be fulfilled: "Not every one who says to me, 'Lord, Lord,' shall enter the kingdom of heaven, but he who does the will of my Father who is in heaven" (Mt. 7, 21ff.).

So, too, the last verse, the statement with which the evangelist

101

closes the discourse (v. 14), becomes comprehensible. A statement of the Lord which originally was addressed to the people of Israel, which differentiates between the summons given to the many—the mass of the people of the covenant—and the "choosing" demonstrated by those who have accepted the Gospel, is here inserted in order to proclaim the analogous truth. The statement could perhaps even be made of the community of disciples, which must let itself be so deeply stirred by the passage that it will not prove true: "For many are called, but few are chosen."

Thus the sermon can be clearly understood. The severity of the prophetic warning is maintained. No Pharisaic consciousness of being called is suffered. All is grace, and all is serious exertion. The call does not cancel out "the fear of the Lord," which is "the beginning of wisdom" (Ps. 111, 10).

IV.

Preparedness

The threatening and warning discourse directed to the people of the covenant is present not only at the beginning of Jesus' prophetic activity; it extends through his entire public life and stands out starkly, as tradition still shows us, once again in the final encounter with the authorities. But it is, in fact, not only those in positions of responsibility who are faced with the decision which is here demanded; the message goes forth to every individual in Israel. Whoever refuses it shares the fate of rejection; whoever accepts and complies with it is singled out of the whole of the people, and there arises the circle of Jesus, the "little flock" who, despite their insignificance, should be without fear, for it has pleased God to give them a share in the coming kingdom (Lk. 12, 32).

The material of the parables which support this summons of the individuals is very rich in the synoptic tradition; basically, it includes everything which is to be treated in the following chapters. A first group can be embraced under the perspective of the admonition that one should not receive the announcement of the event in lazy carelessness. When one hears the message and lets it possess him, his life is opened to the future; whatever he thinks and does, how he understands his existence, what he undertakes and what he suffers in patience, has its meaning and basis in the event which stands there before the door and can enter at any moment. The attitude which corresponds to this expectation is expressly named: it is "watchfulness" in the sense of preparedness. It is this attitude which is demanded by the epigram and driven home in the parable.

The elements to be discussed here indicate especially clearly the connection with the early Christian preaching. That is understandable when one grasps how much the expectation of the final event had characterized the Church of apostolic times. It was known, of course, and again and again as a corrective it was repeated, that no man knows the day and the hour, because it is concealed in God's wisdom (cf. 2 Thes. 2, 1ff.). But the experience of the messianic work and its temporary conclusion was obviously so powerful, and its future completion was fixed so clearly before the eyes of faith, that the blessed desire saw everything within the knowable future with prophetic foreshortening. Thus Paul, probably prompted by an inquiry, could instruct the community at Thessalonica that "we . . . who are left until the coming of the Lord shall not precede those who have fallen asleep" (1 Thes. 4, 15–17). In view of such expectations, the urgent and constantly reiterated warnings for watchfulness explain themselves, as in the same letter: "For you yourselves know well that the day of the Lord will come like a thief in the night. . . . So then let us not sleep, as others do, but let us keep awake and be sober" (5, 2. 6), or in the Letter to the Romans: "Besides this you know what hour it is, how it is full time now for you to wake from sleep. For salvation is nearer to us now than when we first believed; the night is far gone, the day is at hand" (Rom. 13, 11ff.).

If, then, those parables which urged preparedness were favorites of the proclamation, it is comprehensible that they especially have been elaborated upon with allegorical details. The task of discovering the original statement of the Lord and its assertion within this transmitted form becomes even more urgent.

1.

Lk. 12, 39f.:

39 But know this, that if the householder had known at what hour the thief was coming, he should have been awake and would not have left his house to be broken into. [40]You also must be ready; for the Son of man is coming at an hour you do not expect.

If the text is understood as a simple comparison, then the premise and the conclusion do not agree with one another. The conclusion, which has the weight of an express warning, demands unceasing vigilance, giving as a reason that it is not known at what hour the Son of man will come. The premise says something different; this man knows very well the hour. The tension between the two statements dissolves as soon as one sees that it is not a simple comparison which lies before us, but the beginnings of a genuine parable. There is a master of the house; he has noticed or learned through a well-intentioned warning that a plot on his house would be attempted that night. So he commands his servants to hold themselves ready and he himself remains awake, and when the thief comes he is seized. The story is begun but still not worked out; it says only: "if he knew . . . he would have been awake and would not have left his house to be broken into." Once the premise is understood as an undeveloped but genuine parable, then the point of comparison comes into focus. It is grasped with the short statement: "So also must you be ready." But then an independent reason, not taken from the parable, is added to this word of warning: therefore you should be prepared, and unceasingly, because the Parousia of the Son of man will most assuredly come, but no one knows the moment.

105

The form of the story, therefore, although arrested in these beginnings, is already present, and fortunately it is a form that evades every attempt at allegorizing. For in that part which in an allegory would have to be filled by the breakthrough of the kingdom of God made concrete in the Son of man, there stands instead the figure of the thief. And on the other hand, the figure of the master of the house does not point to God or the Son of man—indeed, it is not a typal figure at all!

In the apostolic proclamation the parable is presumed to be familiar. It appears there abbreviated and condensed, and allegorization has come about after all: "The day of the Lord will come like a thief in the night" (1 Thes. 5, 2. 4); "But the day of the Lord will come like a thief" (2 Pt. 3, 10); and still more tersely and sharply: "If you will not awake, *I* will come like a thief, and you will not know at what hour I will come upon you" (Rev. 3, 3), "Lo, I am coming like a thief! Blessed is he who is awake . . ." (Rev. 16, 15). More than ever, it should be noted that in the synoptic tradition the word of the Lord has remained undisturbed.

* * *

In another way it can be compared to the story of the doorkeeper (Mk. 13, 33–37), which is quoted here because of its similarity:

33 Take heed, watch; for you do not know when the time will come. [34]It is like a man going on a journey, when he leaves home and puts his servants in charge, each with his work, and commands the doorkeeper to be on the watch. [35]Watch therefore—for you do not know when the master of the house will come, in the evening, or at midnight, or at cockcrow, or in the morning—[36]lest he come suddenly and find you asleep. [37]And what I say to you I say to all: Watch.

With verse 34 a genuine parable begins. It treats of a man who goes on a journey and entrusts his house and affairs to his servants. Then one of the servants comes to the fore; it is the man who has to watch nights in the gatehouse. He is exhorted to take great care. If this line of thought were carried out, the story might say that one day or night the master returned and found the man at his post, that he praised and rewarded him. The warning would close: So also should you watch and be prepared. . . . From this it can be seen that the story is broken off as soon as the exposition is completed. It was already introduced through the warning (v. 33): ". . . watch; for you do not know when the time will come"; now the warning comes to the fore in its turn and is stated in a similar formulation: "Watch therefore—for you do not know when the master of the house will come, . . . lest he come suddenly and find you asleep" (vv. 35ᵃ, 36). In between, illustrating the "when" there stands the expression "in the evening, or at midnight, or at cockcrow, or in the morning." This is nothing but the popular designation of the four Roman night watches, the same thing that is meant by the "second and third night watch" in the parable of the watching servants (Lk. 12, 38). Thus our attention is guided to the other parable. It tells us: ". . . be like men who are waiting for their master. . . . Blessed are those servants whom the master finds awake when he comes. . . . If he comes in the second watch, or in the third, and finds them so, blessed are those servants!" (Lk. 12, 36ᵃ. 37ᵃ. 38). Now here some details that appeared difficult in the parable of the doorkeeper work in very naturally. For here the master has not gone on a journey, but to a banquet. This explains why he comes home in the night, at a late hour. So it is also comprehensible that on this one night not only the porter, but everyone, even the other servants who have done their work during the day, is awake. But how difficult, on the other hand, is the idea that upon the unexpected return of the master from a long journey all the servants stood ready, watching; for weeks they must neither have slept nights nor have worked days.

So it is obvious to suppose that a transfer has occurred, or to formulate our statement more cautiously, that the warning has been formed according to the model and with the material of the parable of the watchful servants. The parable of the doorkeeper appears submerged in it, although a trace can still be found in the postscript: "lest he come suddenly and find you asleep" (v. 36). So it happens that the remaining fragment supplies only the imagery of the warning. The whole has become a metaphor. In it the few details of the fragment preserve an allegorical meaning. The master who goes on a journey and entrusts his house to the servants and imparts to each his task and his authority portrays Jesus, who before His departure transferred the responsibility for His community to the innermost circle of disciples. Since they are the servants, when the Lord returns in His Parousia, whose mysterious time is the night, He must find not only the doorkeeper but all of them watching. And—so says the sermon—not only them, but all who bear the name of disciples. Therefore, the piece closes with the sentence: "And what I say to you I say to all: Watch."

* * *

A third passage belongs in here. We read it in the version of Matthew (24, 45–51), which agrees almost word for word with that of Luke (12, 41–46) but does not produce the few peripheral sentences in which Luke appears to go beyond the framework of Jesus' sayings.

45 Who then is the faithful and wise servant, whom his master has set over his household, to give them their food at the proper time? [46]Blessed is that servant whom his master when he comes will find so doing. [47]Truly, I say to you, he will set him over all his possessions. *48* But if that wicked servant says to himself, "My master is delayed," [49]and begins to beat his fellow servants, and eats and drinks with the drunken, [50]the master of that servant will come on a day when he does not expect him and at an hour he does not know, [51]and will cut him into pieces, and put him with the hypocrites; there men will weep and gnash their teeth.

The parable has two parts and contrasts two ways of conduct. In the piece discussed earlier, the figure of the doorkeeper stood in the foreground; this time it is the figure of the head servant, under whom the household is placed. Again it is supposed, as the observations on the return show, that the master goes on a journey. So the faithfulness of the servant is put to the test. It proves itself in his righteousness. The lord repays him by making him the administrator of his property. In the counterpart, the servant disregards his duty; he uses the opportunity to domineer the others and enjoy himself capriciously. So he is ruined in the judgment.

In its structure the piece is a pure parable. It is a warning to use earthly time for true service. It sets this life in contrast to the judgment and warns of the foolishness which thinks God is far off and does not see or is not concerned (cf. Ps. 14).

But already an allegorizing explanation is noticeable along the periphery. The story is concluded as clearly as possible with the master, as is his right, having his slave killed; now it is added that "he put him with the hypocrites."[54] That this means a punishment extending beyond death is shown by the addition of Matthew's version: "there men will weep and gnash their teeth." By this the act of punishing in the story is made into a representation of the judgment. And now the explanation reaches farther. The master, who has departed and returned suddenly, to the terror of his servant, "on a day when he does not expect him and at an hour he does not know," is also here the Christ who has departed and appears again to judge. What, then, does the "household" represent? The meaning is obvious, for in the early Christian vocabulary the old biblical words which designated Israel as God's "house" continued to be used (cf. Heb. 3, 6). Now the community of disciples is the "house": "For the time has come for judgment to begin with the household of God; and if it begins *with us,* what will be the end of those who do not obey the gospel of God?" (1 Pt. 4, 17). ". . . you may know how one ought to behave in the household of God, which is the Church of the living God "(1 Tim. 3, 15). If, therefore, the community is the "house," then the servant whom the lord has set over the household for the duration of his absence to give each his bread in justice represents the type of the community head.

With this, the discourse is thematically narrowed and at the same time becomes very "practical." It is a warning to the circle of the "oldest" in the community, and parallels other passages of similar sort. Thus we find in the First Letter of Peter (5, 2ff.): "Tend the flock of God that is your charge not by constraint but willingly, not for shameful gain but eagerly, not as domineering over those in your charge but being examples to the flock." Such warnings only continue what was already said in the words of the Lord: "you know that those who are supposed to rule the

Gentiles lord it over them, and their great men exercise authority over them. But it shall not be so among you; but whoever would be great among you must be your servant, and whoever would be first among you must be slave of all" (Mk. 10, 42–44). Alongside stands the express warning to the heads of the community— and it is not concerned with titles, of course, but with attitudes: "but you are not to be called rabbi, for you have one teacher, and you are all brethren. And call no man your father on earth, for you have one Father, who is in heaven'"; the warning continues with the discussion of the situation of the community: " 'neither be called masters, for you have one master, the Christ" (Mt. 23, 8–10).

The proclaimers know, therefore, of a clear instruction which goes back to Jesus. They are aware of the concern of the Lord lest the circle of disciples decline to the status of the established of the world, and they know that the weak spot is there where authority is given to men.

Luke has gone even further here; from the beginning he concentrates the allegorizing solidly on the community heads. Concerning the two preceding parables, that of the watchful servant (12, 35ff.) and that of the watchful father of the house (12, 39f.), Peter, as spokesman for the twelve, asks: "Lord, are you telling this parable for us or for all?" (12, 41).[55] Jesus does not answer specifically, but he tells the parable of the good and the bad servant. The unspoken answer lies within it: You, whom I have set over my household, you are meant. Luke goes further and draws out of his own special matter the adage in verse 47 of the servant who knows the will of his lord but has not fulfilled it, and this statement is for its part concluded with the sentence:

111

Every one to whom much is given,
  of him will much be required;
and of him to whom men commit much
  they will demand the more.

The examples can teach us that the allegorizing of a parable is no idle game. Through it, that which the careful proclaimers wish to say in the name of the master comes out. To them an exact record of his speech seems less important than to let his word become operative for themselves and the brethren. They restrict themselves to the transmitted parable—it remains recognizable, and no one is forced to understand it allegorically—but they see it in the light of many other things which Jesus said and in the situation which the heavenly Lord brought about through his Spirit.

2.

The parable of the watching servant was already cited in the treatment of the parable of the doorkeeper; now it must be considered more exactly.

Lk. 12, 35–38

35 Let your loins be girded and your lamps burning, [36]and be like men who are waiting for their master to come home from the marriage feast, so that they may open to him at once when he comes and knocks. [37a]Blessed are those servants whom the master finds awake when he comes;

37b truly, I say to you, he will gird himself and have them sit at table, and he will come and serve them.

38 If he comes in the second watch, or in the third, and finds them so, blessed are those servants!

First of all, it must be asked whether a genuine parable lies before us or at least is at the basis of this passage. The newer

112

investigations show a strong tendency to restrict what is accepted as transmitted material; accordingly, one might recognize in the piece not a parable but a metaphorical discourse which arises from the proclamation and proceeds in such a fashion that it unites together the different kinds of statements and parable fragments into a new form, a little sermon with its own theme. So it is conjectured that the stories of the waiting servant and the master of the house who returns home from a banquet—or perhaps, in the full concept of the word "*gamos*," from a wedding celebration—is derived from the parable of the bridesmaids (Mt. 25, 1ff.). On the other hand, it is true that the two pieces really coincide only in that the servants, like the maidens, carried lamps.[56] Or an attempt is made to take the parable of the doorkeeper as the point of departure and to recognize in it the model for that of the waiting servants, or even suppose an ur-form[57] which appears in Mark in the form of the piece on the doorkeeper, in Luke as the servants. All this is of itself possible and defensible, and doubtlessly there is a point of contact between the doorkeeper parable and that of the servants; but it appears more plausible—and that was the point discussed—that the piece of the servants has influenced that of the doorkeeper than vice versa. In any case, it is rewarding to attempt to discover the original parable. Leaving verse 37[b] aside, a clear course appears.

The master of the house has gone to a banquet or wedding dinner. Late in the night, when everything is over, he returns. But not only is the doorkeeper there awake, all his house slaves await him. They stand in the courtyard between the outside gate and the house; they have their robes tucked up in order to open the gate quickly when he knocks, and they carry lamps to illuminate his way into the house. Of course, that is more than service demands; it is an expression of great reverence and attachment. And the lord recognizes the faithfulness and will know how to reward it; it is clear to the hearers that in the end it will be said: "It will be well with those servants." This is certainly no everyday story, but a parable is not limited to that—it can reach out beyond. It is demanded only that the details of the tale remain plausible, and that is here true. Just as once before a servant of reliable faithfulness is described (Mt. 24, 45-47), so here it is a group of men who devote themselves to their lord and are certain of his friendliness. That such a detail is sketched in beyond the intended meaning is not to be denied, but the intended meaning in Jesus' mind is indeed the kingdom, the approach of God, God himself ultimately, the Lord whom one loves "with all his strength." So there is recognizable an independent parable which for the sake of its admonition is put in an imperative form, just as others, for example the piece on the poor servant (Lk. 17, 7-10) or that of the wedding (Mk. 2, 19), were put in an interrogative form.

But when the parable is recognized, the statement left aside at first (v. 37[b]) stands out clearly from its surroundings:

... truly, I say to you, he [the master] will gird himself and have them [the servants] sit at table, and he will come and serve them.

This statement does not have the style of the parable; the proceeding it refers to is not a common or even an uncommon occurrence, but it is nevertheless plausible. None of it is evident from life. The way a lord ordinarily proceeds with his servants, even if he is righteous, was described by Jesus another time: "Will any of you, who has a servant . . . , say to him when he has come in from the field, 'Come at once and sit down at table'?" (Lk. 17, 7). But here the lord does just the opposite; he summons his servants to recline at table, and he himself waits on them. The conception, which is deliberately paradoxical, stems from its own context which has nothing to do with the parable. It is found in a group of statements with which Jesus carefully disclosed the mystery which ordains His life and becomes manifest in His death.

The tradition of Luke has placed one of these within the frame of the Last Supper in order to disclose its meaning: "For which is the greater, one who sits at table, or one who serves? Is it not the one who sits at table? But I am among you as one who serves" (Lk. 22, 27).[58] How strongly this passage has determined the insight of the disciples can be shown in the fourth Gospel. For John, the love which humbles itself by serving shows forth in the foot-washing which takes place in the middle of the Last Supper (Jn. 13, 1ff.). What was in Luke a brief statement has now become a whole treatment, and what is done becomes a significant *mysterium:* the service unto death of the Son of God is here present and effective.

In the chain of aphorisms transmitted by Luke, the passage of the serving lord is followed by one in which Jesus promises the disciples that when the kingdom of God has come and the messianic dominion is established, they should eat and drink at His table (Lk. 22, 30; cf. 22, 18). Here the presentation of the eschatological meal of consummation (cf. Mt. 8, 11) is concretized in the meal which the Exalted One will hold with His own.

This knowledge teaches us how to understand the form and the meaning of the passage which has been assimilated into the parable. Now it is told in the third person that the lord, having returned home, will bid his faithful servants to recline at table and wait upon them.

Without doubt, the course of the parable's story is confused through the interpolation. The master, after all, has an extended banquet behind him; thus it is incongruent if another is held, especially in the middle of the night and without time for preparation. But such inconsistencies are not disturbing, because the discourse is already understood allegorically; the course on the plane of spiritual meaning moves without break.

If one acknowledges the right of the proclaimers to their own discourse, then one hears a sermon of sublime beauty and winning strength. One sees how the servants await their lord in loving preparedness, and remembers the beseeching cry of the disciples: *"Maranatha* —O Lord, come" (1 Cor. 16, 22; Rev. 22, 17; Didache 10, 6). One hears the returning master knock at the gate and thinks of what the author of Revelation has heard: "Behold, I stand at the door and knock; if any one hears my voice and opens the door, I will come in to him and eat with him, and he with me" (Rev. 3, 20). One sees the servants who have girded themselves in order to be quick to hurry out and loose the heavy bolt, sees them greet the lord and with their lamps light his way into the house. One perceives how he now treats his own, how he leads them into the upper chamber and the dinner is ready at once and the hall shines forth with light in the middle of the night. One recognizes that here is the fulfillment of the passage which the Lord had spoken before He went forth to His passion: "that you may eat and drink at my table in my kingdom . . ." (Lk. 22, 30). And then the mystery of that meal reveals itself: in an incomprehensible reversal the servants are made lords, and the lord makes himself a servant.

116

Thus does the love which surpasses all imagination answer the meager, modest love of the disciples. With this image the discourse stops; it dies away in praising the blessed who are prepared at every hour.

3.

The parable of the waiting servants is transmitted only by Luke; Matthew brings into the same context the parable of the bridesmaids instead. It is possible that already in the available tradition sometimes the one, sometimes the other was given preference. That is understandable, for even if the plot and characters of the two are so different that neither of them can be derived from the other, it is nevertheless conceivable that in preaching one could replace the other. For the sermon finds in each of them its one enveloping theme; on the other hand, with the differing layout of the two exegetical observation might expect to find even a different assertion or a differently accentuated one.

MT. 25, 1–13:

1 Then the kingdom of heaven shall be compared to ten maidens who took their lamps and went to meet the bridegroom. [2]Five of them were foolish, and five were wise. [3]For when the foolish took their lamps, they took no oil with them; [4]but the wise took flasks of oil with their lamps.

5 As the bridegroom was delayed, they all slumbered and slept. [6]But at midnight there was a cry, "Behold, the bridegroom! Come out to meet him." [7]Then all those maidens rose and trimmed their lamps. [8]And the foolish said to the wise, "Give us some of your oil, for our lamps are going out." [9]But the wise replied, "Perhaps there will not be enough for us and for you; go rather to the dealers and buy for yourselves."

10 And while they went to buy, the bridegroom came, and those

117

who were ready went in with him to the marriage feast; and the door was shut.

11 Afterward the other maidens came also, saying, "Lord, lord, open to us." [12]But he replied, "Truly, I say to you, I do not know you."

13 Watch therefore, for you know neither the day nor the hour.

A significant group of exegetes is inclined or completely determined to explain this discourse as completely allegorical; in conformity with the assumption that Jesus himself formed no allegories, but also from internal evidence, they recognize it as a product of the proclamation. Here there is portrayed, it is said, a procedure which does not agree with the actual wedding customs of the time and surroundings of Jesus. So it must be assumed that here it is not intended that an incident from this life lead by virtue of its own logic to a deeper insight, as happens in a genuine parable; rather, an assertion of faith is imbedded in single "snapshots" which do not hang together of themselves but are brought to an artificial unity only by the governing idea.[59] Others see in the piece a support for the assertion that the delay of the Parousia must not lessen the hoping expectation and constant vigilance; they therefore recognize a genuine parable, but because of its theme they do not accept it as the word of Jesus.[60]

So we must begin with the tale and ask whether it is thinkable that its course was plausible to the first hearers. The question must be played so cautiously because we are not—or not yet— capable of clearly reconstructing for ourselves the wedding customs in the environment of Jesus. It cannot be said with certainty, therefore, that the plot presented is true to life, nor can one affirm that it contradicts the customs. That the course of events, as it is described or intimated or presumed, is credible, is supported by occasional assertions in the rabbinical documents as well as by usages observed even today by Jews and Arabs.[61]

From these we see that the wedding is normally held in the house of the bridegroom or of his father. The bride waits in her parental house until the bridegroom comes with his friends to fetch her and to lead her in a festive procession to his house, where the blessing of the marriage and the wedding banquet take place.[62]

Despite many variations in detail reflecting family and district, the customs of today coincide with the old customs.[63] It is important to note that the arrival of the bridegroom is awaited until late at night, that he is announced by messengers, that his appearance leads to the first high point of the celebration: the meeting of bridegroom and bride and the joyful procession, illuminated by torches and lamps, to the wedding house. That the meeting of bridegroom and bride could be seen as an incident susceptible to allegorical interpretation is shown even in ancient times by a rabbinical exegesis to Ex. 19, 17: "Then Moses brought the people out of the camp to meet God. . . ." To this it is said: "Moses went out into the camp of the Israelites and awakened them from their sleep: Arise from your sleep, already the bridegroom comes and desires his bride, to lead her into the bridal chamber. . . ." And to the text from Deuteronomy: "The Lord came from Sinai, and dawned from Seir upon us; he shone forth from Mount Paran, . . . Yea, he loved his people; . . . as a possession for the assembly of Jacob" (Dt. 33, 2. 3. 4), another exegesis says: "He came in order to receive Israel like a bridegroom who goes to meet the bride."[64]

The feature which is so important for the parable, the delay in the arrival of the bridegroom, is a ritual affair. It heightens the expectation by means of delays, and the announcement of the coming, given once or even several times at intervals, creates a tension which is released with the entrance in triumphant joy of the event whose full meaning is also thereby experienced.[65]

In such a plot-scheme the details of the parable tale appear to be in proper order. They do not—and this must be noted and not lost sight of—describe the wedding itself, but only an incident in its periphery. The figures who perform here and who reap the consequences of their actions are only the ten maidens who belong to the train of the bride and wait at her house for the beginning of the celebration. There is no talk of the bride. Indeed, she plays no role in this peripheral action. But even the bridegroom does not really stand in focus. To be exact, it is not he but his approach that is concerned, for with this there begins the service for which the bridesmaids are appointed. They must go to meet him and his companions, conduct them to the bride, and then, surrounding the bride, proceed with the festive procession to the house of the bridegroom and into the wedding hall. Only at the very end of the story does the bridegroom stand out actively, and there is a special reason for that.

Now it is said of the bridesmaids that there were prudent and foolish among them. But what it means to be prudent or foolish must be recognized from the conduct of the two groups.

It is said of all that they fall asleep during the long wait. It is understandable that they let their lamps burn, for it is bothersome to put out the fire and then light it up again. But as a result, at the decisive moment the wicks are sooted and the oil runs short. It is therefore necessary to clean the lamps quickly and replenish the oil, and now the circumspection of the one stands the test, and the lack of foresight of the other is punished.

Thus a personal attitude is made visible in a practical procedure. Of course, this parable, unlike that of the servants, is not concerned with being awake in contrast to sleeping, for all had fallen asleep, and now all are awake. The difference had already occurred at the beginning. All wished to be there at the reception of the bridegroom and the splendid celebration—the hearers understand this well, for, like people everywhere, they love weddings. But, the parable says, he who wishes to be present without fail at the great moment must also do everything to be prepared. It is not sufficient to make halfway, frivolous preparations with the idea that one's exertions will certainly be enough. What is demanded is a preparation seriously resolved upon, reckoning with every possibility, paying every price.

At this point the tale could end. It needs only to be said that, as the story continues, the foolish with their quenched lamps are shamed before everyone and excluded from the celebration. But the treatment is set into motion anew. The unfortunate bridesmaids attempt to get aid for themselves. They run to the house of the shopkeeper and knock and call to awaken him, but this takes time, and they miss the entrance for which they have waited so long.

But that is not all; they are completely excluded from the celebration. The story has withdrawn them from the scene in order to let them enter again only when the wedding procession has arrived at the house and the crowd of guests has entered and the gate of the courtyard, as the late hour demands, is closed and bolted.

This is an impressive conclusion. But one understands that in the version handed down this scene is now heightened intensely. The unfortunate call out in their despair to the bridegroom; they call him "*Kyrios* — Lord" and beg beseechingly: "Open to us!"

But once closed, the door is not to be opened again—actually a proverbial expression for "Too late!"[66] The answer of the lord, too, is a statement of rejection: "I do not know you" (cf. Mt. 7, 23), and this in its turn is bound up with the adjuring formula of the "Amen" used here, which is characteristic of the speaking style of Jesus.[67] Here the language is clearly no longer on the level of parable, but direct. Words of the judging Son of man are placed in the mouth of the bridegroom.

A further reflection confirms this perception. According to the synoptic tradition, Jesus has neither taken over and developed the Old Testament prophetic theme of betrothal between Yahweh and Israel (cf., for example, Jos. 2, 21f.; Jer. 2, 2; 12, 7; Ez. 16, 8) as such nor in any way applied it to the Messiah. Thus the community of disciples is never presented as a type of the bride; at most the disciples are understood as the guests at that wedding banquet in whose image the messianic time of salvation is comprehended.

The early proclamation speaks much differently. Now it is recognized that God has appointed His Messiah as a mediator of the covenant, and that the "kernel" and "remnant" of Israel remains and carries this summons further, so that in the relationship between the glorified Christ and the hallowed Church the marriage bond between Yahweh and Israel gains a new and more compact form. Now it can be said, as Paul says, "I betrothed you to Christ to present you as a pure bride to her one husband" (2 Cor. 11, 2). ". . . as Christ loved the church and gave himself up for her, that he might sanctify her, . . . that the church might be presented before him in splendor, without spot or wrinkle or any such thing . . ." (Eph. 5, 25–27). Now the Baptist in the Gospel of John can say prophetically: "He who has the bride is the bridegroom; the friend of the bridegroom, who stands and hears him, rejoices greatly at the bridegroom's voice . . ." (Jn. 3, 29). But the prophet of the Apocalypse gazes upon the end: ". . . for the marriage of the Lamb has come, and his Bride has made herself ready . . ." (Rev. 19, 7; cf. 21, 1. 9; 22, 17).

If the material and the means by which it is bound to the transmitted matter to achieve such an intensification are questioned, a possible model appears in a statement of the Lord coming from the special matter of Luke, an image in which some suspect the fragment of a lost parable:[68] "When once the householder has risen up and shut the door, you will begin to stand outside and to knock at the door, saying, 'Lord, open to us.' He will answer you, 'I do not know where you come from.' Then you will begin to say, 'We ate and drank in your presence, and you taught in our streets.' But he will say, 'I tell you, I do not know where you come from; depart form me, all you workers of iniquity!' " (Lk. 13, 25–27).

But if, as the passages cited from Paul and John show, the holy betrothal of the heavenly Lord and His earthly community is spoken of, a statement of the Lord containing a wedding and a wedding feast, at least in the background, cannot remain, so to speak, untilled. The proclamation takes possession of it. It does not destroy the structure; it is content that in the end, where the parable requires an application, the intensification succeeds. For at this point the hearer is led to an understanding of the entire discourse that settles like a second layer over the original tale. Thus Christ is now from the beginning the bridegroom, and His coming is awaited. That He fails to appear for a long time and then arrives suddenly points to the uncertainty of the day and the hour when "the Son of man is coming" (Mt. 24, 44; cf. Rev.

16, 15; 1 Thes. 5, 2. 4; etc.).[69] It is unfortunate—but as a matter of fact such things often happen to an allegorical interpretation —that the bride is not named. But her bridesmaids can stand in her place. Their number, and not least their different bearings, make it easy to think of the multitude of disciples. The act of meeting now appears to be of the greatest significance. With the burning lamps, with the light which is the sign of vocation, the disciples who have loyally awaited the Parousia walk to meet the Lord. He leads them into the hall of the heavenly wedding and to the meal of consummation, and they "may eat and drink at his table in his kingdom" (Lk. 22, 30). But those who did not stand ready with lamps burning are rejected. So the discourse consists of threat and promise and, despite the horrible conclusion, lays perhaps the greater weight on the promise. In any case, now, unlike in the original parable, the future event stands in focus. The dominant image is that of the blessed marriage. For its sake and from it arises the warning formulated by the added concluding statement (v. 13): "Watch therefore, for you know neither the day nor the hour."

V.

The Contribution

The situation originating with the appearance of Jesus brings God's claim to the service of Israel, which had been raised for a long time, to a point of highest urgency. The order of the law, which had given it form, is now intrinsically exceeded. The individual is challenged and from him there is demanded a contribution to the affairs of God which can no longer be expressed in the decrees of the law. This is the insight which is contained in the passage in Luke's tradition (16, 16):

The law and the prophets were until John; since then the good news of the kingdom of God is preached, and every one enters it violently.

"Every one enters it violently"—in this way the prophetic style presents as fact what at another time sounds like a warning:

Strive to enter by the narrow door; for many, I tell you, will seek to enter and will not be able (Lk. 13, 24).

A similar dictum is transmitted by Matthew, an emphatic passage of great boldness, which must not be weakened in translation:

From the days of John the Baptist until now the kingdom of heaven has suffered violence, and men of violence take it by force (Mt. 11, 12).[70]

The boldness lies in speaking of the sovereignty of God as something that can be taken by force. Everyone in the circle of

Jesus knows that such a passivity is unthinkable of God. But the passage is indeed ironic; the notion that salvation can be possessed by force is permitted to arise calmly and continue to exist only in order to express very clearly that a contribution which goes all the way is demanded of men. A series of parables treats of this.

1.

LK. 14, 28–32:

28 For which of you, desiring to build a tower, does not first sit down and count the cost, whether he has enough to complete it? ²⁹Otherwise, when he had laid a foundation, and is not able to finish, all who see it begin to mock him, ³⁰saying, "This man began to build, and was not able to finish."

The discourse begins in the form of a question; the hearers are challenged to judge themselves. Some among them would themselves like to erect such a "tower" in their vineyard, or a barn with a rock substructure outside on the field. But what good is the wish? Only a fool will build without first determining how much there is to spend.

31 Or what king, going to encounter another king in war, will not sit down first and take counsel whether he is able with ten thousand to meet him who comes against him with twenty thousand? ³²And if not, while the other is yet a great way off, he sends an embassy and asks terms of peace.

The two pieces are bound together in the form of a double parable. Both say the same thing. What is true for the little farmers is also true for the great king. What is for one the tower is victory for the other.[71]

Ostensibly, there is an alternative presented here: either one risks the large undertaking, in which case a sufficient contribution

must be produced, or one relinquishes the plan from the first.[72]
But such an either-or is really not offered; it is valid only in the
scope of the story. The decision in the affair which Jesus had in
mind is certainly not left to one's option. The decision, therefore,
concerns the contribution. The discourse exacts a consequence;
it demands that it be begun correctly, somewhat in the sense of
the text: "No one who puts his hand to the plow and looks back
is fit for the kingdom of God" (Lk. 9, 62). So the double parable
stands near to the parable of building a house (Mt. 7, 24ff.). The
intimation which is made here in the deplorable miscarrying of
the undertaking becomes in the other parable a clear indication
of the catastrophe of the judgment: under the storm tide the
house collapses.

The meaning of the parable may originally have been clear
through its position in the eschatological proclamation of Jesus.
It did not need a concluding sentence to point to the kingdom of
God. Instead there is the dictum:

33 So therefore, whoever of you does not renounce all that he has
cannot be my disciple.

This may not be considered in isolation, for it belongs in the
context of the concluding proverbs which precede the double
parable: Lk. 14, 25–27. That it is not brought out there, but only
after the parable, reveals an artistic skill; the parable and the
group of proverbs are meant to be bracketed together as tightly
as possible.[73] This passage exhibits a radicalism which is not
found anywhere else in the words of the Lord. But because the
double parable gets its "application" from the group of proverbs,
which in turn strives to acquire its impact from the double
parable, the question of how such a formulation came about must

be pursued. And because in line with this technique of bracketing it is to be expected that the concluding epigram condenses the assertion of what has gone before, these must be considered more exactly.

The passage deals with the decision for discipleship; obedience to the Gospel is effected by the union to Jesus, which it proclaims. This happens in various ways. To "follow" Jesus means first of all very literally that one, as custom demands of the students of scholars, "walk behind him." But because Jesus entered as a prophet, those studying under Him also partake of the prophetic commission; He sends them "ahead of him, two by two," and gives them power over the unclean spirits and so they set forth and summon to conversion, proclaim the message, and heal (Mk. 6, 7. 12f.; Lk. 9, 1–2. 6; 10, 1. 9). The disciple did not of himself resolve on such a following; he was summoned and called to it (Mk. 1, 17f.; 2, 14; Lk. 5, 11; 9, 59; etc.). There does not thus originate a better and real discipleship, but actually a form of accomplishment of discipleship ordained by God's decree.[74]

Its fundamental law is in the compilation of dicta formulated in Mk. 8, 34–38 = Lk. 9, 23–26. It demands that one surrender his earthly existence—"let him deny himself"—and be prepared to take upon himself the death of disgrace, the gallows of the "cross"; that he comprehend that deliverance in the future can be accomplished only by an honest exchange; he does not cling to his life, but stakes it, and God himself rescues it. But if the decision in favor of discipleship means so much, then being called to the circle of those who go about with Jesus adds nothing of meaning. Thus it comes about that the concept of "follower" could

128

be extended to the broad circle of those who accepted Jesus and His Gospel. Such a proceeding is legitimate.

Nevertheless, the fundamental discipleship becomes visible in the life pattern of those who partake of the prophetic work, and therefore the passages which refer to it, have significance for all disciples. Perhaps this is the reason that those passages addressed to the group who travelled with Jesus and those addressed to the broader circle often stand alongside one another without differentiation and, as the group of dicta in 14, 25-27 shows, even penetrate one another. So there occurs a passage on the fundamental discipleship which speaks of the bitter dissension which the Gospel brings into families: "Do you think that I have come to give peace on earth? No, I tell you, but rather division; for henceforth in one house there will be five divided, three against two and two against three . . . , father against son and son against father, mother against daughter and daughter against her mother . . ." (Lk. 12, 51-53 = Mt. 10, 34-36[Q]). But in close proximity to it there is also a text to the men whom the prophetic commission has separated from home and family, from possessions and profession, and displaced into an insecure existence. In the synoptic tradition it is found annexed to the report of the ineffectual calling of the rich young man to service (Mk. 10, 17ff.). Peter, as spokesman of the twelve, says: "Lo, we have left our homes and followed you." Jesus answers: "Truly, I say to you, there is no man who has left house or wife or brothers or children, for the sake of the kingdom of God, who will not receive manifold more in this time, and in the age to come eternal life" (Lk. 18, 28ff.).

Now it can be seen what has happened in the group of dicta. To begin with, these very words of the Lord are used, but now they are no longer addressed to the men in the narrowest circle, but to a "numerous throng," which evidently represent the broad circle of followers. An important insertion is made. After saying, "If any one comes to me and does not hate his own father and mother ["hate" is used here in the Semitic manner of speaking: to neglect or treat another slightingly[75]] and wife and children and brothers and sisters," the passage suddenly expands, "yes, and even his own life," and then concludes, "he cannot be my disciple." The enlargement obviously wishes to recall the text which demands that one give up his life (Mk. 8, 35 = Lk. 9, 24). But that spoke of the fundamental discipleship, just as what immediately follows: "Whoever does not bear his own cross and come after me, cannot be my disciple." One sees that here there are twined together two texts which were originally separated because they were addressed to different hearers. But that means that challenges which arise meaningfully out of the special situation of the "followers" are generalized and raised before men who are not in the same situation at all.

When now, in accord with the technique of bracketing, there is produced after the double parable the epigram in which those preceding the parable are condensed, the impression of a rigorous radicalism arises; for now it says: "So therefore, *whoever* of you does not renounce *all* that he has cannot be my disciple." The verse evidently pleased the evangelist, for he has an "ideal" of poverty. This is expressed in many places.[76] The passage closest to that discussed here is Luke's version of the treasure-hoarding. In the parallel in Mt. 6, 19ff. it is merely stated: "Do not lay up for yourselves treasures on earth . . . but lay up for yourselves treasures in heaven . . ."; in Luke the dictum begins with the words: "Sell your possessions, and give alms . . ." (12, 33). Here not only is the desire to amass riches rejected, but it is demanded that one voluntarily make himself poor. Perhaps this also contains a challenge to the "followers," which grows out of their service and results in an austere concept which is extended to the fundamental discipleship. When it is said to the rich young man that he should exchange his possessions for money and distribute his money to the poor, the challenge corresponds to the situation; but if such a thing is demanded of all disciples, then this special case is made a norm, and the impression is formed that to be without possessions is necessary for salvation. That Luke is really presenting no such radicalism in all his appraisals of poverty is shown in the presentation of the original community which he gives in the first chapters of the Acts. There can be no talk of a poverty necessary in principle there.

The example demonstrates anew how a parable has in composition been placed within a thematic important to preaching. If it is removed and again given the breadth it had in the seminal proclamation of Jesus, then the strength of the discourse will be revealed. It stands in the powerful tension between the future event and the present hour. The claim upon men which God will carry through in the judgment is already raised here and now in the Gospel, and a decision is demanded. A share in the kingdom, life in the era of the consummation, can be won or lost. He who wishes to win it must know its worth and produce the price. The prophetic words destroy the illusions of those who believe they can idly let the future come to them, that their being children of Abraham will identify them before the judgment court (Mt. 3, 9; 8, 11). But it also warns the disciples, for the decision cannot happen once for all; it must be carried through in ever new trials in the fabric of life "to the very end" (cf. Mt. 10, 22).

131

2.

Considered in itself, the double parable has said nothing more than that a full contribution is necessary to attain the future goals. What is now to be treated states more clearly how such a contribution is to be understood, at what place it is to be accomplished, and how it can be tainted. It is doubtlessly pertinent to the clearer understanding of the assertion to note that the early Christian proclamation has again, and indeed more strongly than in any of the previously discussed pieces, been deposited upon the precise text. If both the assertion of Jesus and that of the proclaimer are to be in focus, a few exertions will be necessary.

The parable of the talents transmitted by Matthew has its parallel in that of the pounds to be found in Luke. So it must be asked first of all whether we are dealing with parables independent of one another or a single parable transmitted in different versions. It would be helpful to place them alongside one another.

Mt. 25, 14–30	Lk. 19, 11–27
	11 . . . He proceeded to tell a parable, because he was near to Jerusalem, and because they supposed that the kingdom of God was to appear immediately.
14 It will be [with the kingdom of heaven: 25, 1] as when a man going on a journey	*12* He said therefore, "A nobleman went into a far country to receive kingly power and then return.
called his servants and entrusted to them his property; ¹⁵to one he gave five talents, to another two, to another one, to each according to his ability. Then he went away.	*13* Calling ten of his servants, he gave them ten pounds, and said to them, 'Trade with these till I come.'

132

16 He who had received the five talents went at once and traded with them; and he made five talents more. [17]So too, he who had the two talents made two talents more. [18]But he who had received the one talent, went and dug in the ground and hid his master's money.

19 Now after a long time the master of those servants came and settled accounts with them.

20 And he who had received the five talents came forward, bringing five talents more, saying, 'Master, you delivered to me five talents; here I have made five talents more.'

21 His master said to him, 'Well done, good and faithful servant; you have been faithful over a little, I will set you over much; enter into the joy of your master.'

22 And he also who had the two talents came forward, saying, 'Master, you delivered to me two talents; here I have made two talents more.'

14 But his citizens hated him and sent an embassy after him, saying, 'We do not want this man to reign over us.'

15 When he returned, having received the kingly power, he commanded these servants, to whom he had given the money, to be called to him, that he might know what they had gained by trading.

16 The first came before him, saying, 'Lord, your pound has made ten pounds more.'

17 And he said to him, 'Well done, good servant! Because you have been faithful in a very little, you shall have authority over ten cities.'

18 And the second came, saying, 'Lord, your pound has made five pounds.'

133

23 His master said to him, 'Well done, good and faithful servant; you have been faithful over a little, I will set you over much; enter into the joy of your master.'

24 He also who had received the one talent came forward, saying, 'Master,
I knew you to be a hard man, reaping where you did not sow, and gathering where you did not winnow;

25 so I was afraid, and I went and hid your talent in the ground. Here you have what is yours.'

26 But his master answered him, 'You wicked and slothful servant! You knew that I reap where I have not sowed, and gather where I have not winnowed? *27*Then you ought to have invested my money with the bankers, and at my coming I should have received what was my own with interest.

28 So take the talent from him, and give it to him who has the ten talents.

29 For to every one who has will be given, and he will have abundance; but from him who has not, even what he has will be taken away.

19 And he said to him, 'And you are to be over five cities.'

20 Then another came, saying, 'Lord, here is your pound, which I kept laid away in a napkin;

21 for I was afraid of you, because you are a severe man; you take up what you do not lay down, and reap what you did not sow.'

22 He said to him, 'I will condemn you out of your own mouth, you wicked servant! You knew that I was a severe man, taking up what I did not lay down and reaping what I did not sow? *23*Why then did you not put my money into the bank, and at my coming I should have collected it with interest?

24 And he said to those who stood by, 'Take the pound from him, and give it to him who has the ten pounds.'

25 And they said to him, 'Lord, he has ten pounds!'

26 'I tell you, that to every one who has will more be given; but from him who has not, even what he has will be taken away.

30 And cast the worthless servant into the outer darkness;
there men will weep and gnash
their teeth.' . . ."

27 But as for these enemies of
mine, who did not want me to
reign over them, bring them
here and slay them before me.' "

To those unpracticed in synoptic observation, the relation of the
two texts will remain unclear at first. But the task of exegesis lies
in precisely that which at first appears confused. So it is well to
elucidate the structure of both through a schema which will show
where the versions coincide and where they diverge. The texts
will be called into memory through catch-words.

Mt. 25, 14–30	Lk. 19, 12–27
14 a man	*12* a man of noble birth in a strange land kingly power
15 to the first servant 5 talents, the second 2, the third 1 (1 talent is about a thousand dollars)	*13* to each servant 1 pound (1 pound is about twenty dollars)
16–18 The first and second double their sum. The third buries the money.	
	14 the attempt to prevent his becoming king
19 the return of the master and the reckoning (15)	
20–23 The report of the two servants.	*16–19* The report of the two servants.
Reward: the joy of the lord	The first: increased the one pound to ten; Reward: 10 cities. The second: increased the one pound to five; Reward: 5 cities.

the third servant

24–25 Out of fear of the strict master he has (20–21) hidden
(guarded) the money and returns it as it was.
26–27 condemnation of the servant (22–23)
28 punishment: the preserved money is (24–25) taken
from him and given to the first.
29 concluding dictum: "every one who has . . ." (26)
30 expulsion of the servant
"into the outer darkness."

27 Judgment on the opposition.

The schema itself makes available a few observations which can
be fruitful for exegesis.

If one recalls the parables treated up till now, there appears a
rule which orders the tales: their line intensifies; the weight of
the treatment along with the pivot of the parable always lies at
the end. So one can speak of the chief act of the plot and of the
"preliminary story," which usually leads tersely and teleologically
to the climax. Now a consideration of this diagram shows that
the climax lies in the dialogue between the lord and the third
servant; everything else, such as the surrender of monies and even
the settling of accounts with the first and second servant, belongs
to the preliminaries.

The diagram further shows that while the two versions diverge
widely in the preliminary story, in the presentation of the climax
they agree almost word for word. So it is to be assumed that here
the original discourse is manifest, while the rest is overlaid with
some secondary assertions.

The question which of the two versions takes precedence of
age is an improper one. For a spare and simple preliminary story
need only tell that a man who wished to go on a trip had made
over his cash to his domestic slaves in the expectation that they
would trade with it. A group of them had taken pains for the
affairs of their master with zeal and success, but another had

given back the money at his return just as it was, without decrease and without increase. That is sufficient to introduce the climax. So again the twofold task presents itself: to discover the original discourse and its intention in the section beginning with the dialogue with the third servant, and then, the second time through, to recognize the assertions of the individual proclaimers which from time to time show through in both versions.

The schema also shows that the parable is terminated with the maxim-type epigram: "Every one who has. . . ." In the text of Luke this is evident, but Matthew, too, does not contradict it: he adds only the actual punishment which obviously and with good reason seemed to him lacking in his model text. For this he has the formula which also forms the conclusion of the parable fragment of the wedding garment (22, 13).

But if the epigram concludes the parable, the question immediately arises whether it belongs to the original text or is added in composition. This second alternative is to be accepted. We have here an independent statement which can be applied meaningfully in more than one place; thus it is also found in the chain of epigrams which is attached to the explanation of the parables of sowing (Mk. 4, 25). In addition several examples show that the transmitters, and originally, we dare say, the preachers, are inclined to conclude parables with just such statements of universal value. The parable of the banquet in the Matthew version says, "For many are called, but few are chosen" (22, 14); the parable of the maidens, "Watch therefore, for you know neither the day nor the hour" (25, 13); the parable of the master of the laborers, which has already been compared, "So the last will be first, and the first last" (20, 16). Such is also the function of the statement, "To every one who has will more be given. . . ."

137

But because the presentation of the decree of punishment in Matthew, verse 28, and Luke, verses 24f., seems influenced by the epigram—and that must be shown later, exegesis must concentrate first of all only on the dialogue, that in Matthew, verses 24–27, and Luke, verses 20–23.

The servant who is here brought to account has not expressly refused his duty. He was not even simply lazy, for it is only Matthew in verse 26 who brings in such an ethical evaluation; his failure to act has another basis. The man was inactive to a shocking degree. He did not do the least thing for the affairs of his lord. He did not even entrust the money to the banker so that it could bring interest. And just such an action would indeed have been preferred by the lazy; it would have been more comfortable than, as Matthew says, to bury the money in the field. So it was not laziness, it was a crippling anxiety: "So I was afraid, and I went and hid your talent in the ground" (Mt., v. 25).[77] According to the purpose of the presentation, the hearer should perceive that the man feels in a desperate way in the right when he again places the very coins which he had received into the hand of his lord. To be sure, he had failed to act and had dashed the expectations of his lord; but what kind of lord is it—in this the salient point becomes apparent—of whom one can say with the proverb that he harvests where he did not sow. The phrase characterizes a tyrant before whose sudden and incomprehensible outbursts one must defend himself.

So it is a heavy misfortune and a genuine catastrophe when the lord in his anger manifests the severity which the servant had eloquently depicted and repulses the desperate.

So much for the story. What does it represent? That it speaks of the relationship to God is obvious. The very figures of the lord and the servants, the expectation of service and the typical proceeding of settling the account along with reward and punishment, all point to this. But just because of all this is it important to perceive that the story does go deeper and does not remain on the plane of ethical conduct. It describes not a wanton sloth, but the inactivity of a man who does not understand his master, and who is, therefore, incapable of love and its deeds; or to express this idea differently, we might say that the parable concerns not good and evil, but folly and wisdom, that which is right and that which is fundamentally perverted.[78]

* * *

If in order to confirm the understanding of the discourse, we explore the situation in which it occurs, and learn that the discourse is listened to in connection with similar sounding statements of Jesus, then we will be able to conclude that it is the doctrine of justification of the Pharisees that was in mind all the while. In the confrontation Jesus says: "This people honors me with their lips, but their heart is far from me; in vain do they worship me, teaching as doctrines the precepts of men" (Mt. 15, 8-9). The doctrine is condemned because it does not observe the real demand of God: "Woe to you . . . , for you tithe mint and dill and cummin, and have neglected the weightier matters of the law, justice and mercy and faith; . . . You blind guides, straining out a gnat and swallowing a camel!" (Mt. 23, 23ff.; cf. Lk. 11, 42). It is condemned as erroneous: "But woe to you . . . because you shut the kingdom of heaven against men; for you neither enter yourselves, nor allow those who would enter to go in" (Mt. 23, 13). Here judgment is pronounced on a piety which lays an unbearable burden upon itself and others with its countless precepts, and yet with all these cannot find grace with God (Mt. 23, 4).[79]

The opposition between what Jesus meant by the fulfillment of the will of God and what the Pharisees understood by the phrase is apparent in the question of healing on the sabbath. Of course, the scribes know that the validity of the commandment of the sabbath rest is limited by the necessities of life—Jesus reminds them of this fact: "Does each of you on the sabbath untie his ox or his ass from the manger, and lead it away to water it?" (Lk. 13, 15); —but such a restriction is again only the result of a legal release and not of a direct insight into the will of God. Jesus, on the other hand, is led by the recognition of a demand which is stronger than the cult of law and all prescriptions which surround it. The sabbath means to Him a manifestation of the benevolence of God towards His creature, and the sabbath rest means peace and happiness. He therefore asks His adversaries, who consider Him a violator of the sabbath: "Is it lawful on the sabbath to do good or to do harm, to save life or to kill?" (Mk. 3, 4; cf. Lk. 13, 16).

When the parable is placed within the controversy, it is seen that it is Pharisaical piety which is rejected in a veiled but nevertheless clear manner in the dialogue with the servant. Anyone who takes upon himself the countless prescriptions with which the scribes (as they themselves sometimes say) have drawn a "fence" around the commandments of the Mosaic law, has neither the watchfulness nor the freedom of movement to recognize and to do the living will of God, which reveals itself spontaneously and is not to be grasped in letters. But if it is explained that this very binding to the service of the law is indeed the will of God, then the parable tells us that precisely in this concept is the image of God distorted; now He actually appears to be an intractable, enigmatical, and dangerous tyrant, and one does well to risk nothing and to develop no personal initiative.[80]

At bottom, then, the parable concerns the recognition of God, a knowledge that proceeds from the attitude which Jesus calls "faith." This is the point of deepest opposition between Him and the scribes. It is a distorted image of God which imprisons man in the law and obstructs his view of what is happening in front of him; one thinks of the meeting of Jesus with the Pharisee Simon, who does not understand what moves the sinner to wash the feet of the prophet with her tears (Lk. 7, 36ff.). It is ignorance of the mind of God which gives the legalists their cold severity and makes them unmerciful, zealous judges who understand nothing of pity and atonement, of forbearance and love, and take scandal when Jesus lets the sinners come to Him and even eats with them (Lk. 15, 1; 19, 7; etc.).

Now the challenge which the parable supports becomes clear: whoever fears God and loves Him must come forth out of his anxious security and confidently follow the directions of His will; he must make the concerns of God his own and therein manifest the courage which matches the magnanimity of God.

3.

The assertion of the parable was discerned from the dialogue alone; now the rest of the text must be examined.

The dialogue was concluded with the censorious question: "Why then did you not put my money into the bank?" The enactment of punishment which then follows (Mt., v. 28; Lk., v. 24) consists in both versions in that the badly managed money is

141

taken from the servant and given to the first in addition to his reward. But here discrepancies are found. How does it happen that the men who as slaves could only earn profits for their master now may retain the confided money along with the profits? In Luke, the detail is still to some extent understandable, for the small sum of less than twenty-five dollars might indeed be given as a trial for a greater task and as such not have been considerable for the great master. In Matthew, however, the first is permitted to retain the five talents which were entrusted to him along with the five which he earned, and over and above he gains the one talent of the man condemned. Here the original layer of the tale appears to have fallen out of view. But the discrepancy also shows itself in the version of Luke: what can it mean to a man who has just been made the governor over a ten-city area if another twenty-five dollars is given him? It must also strike one that the second servant, who according to Matthew did perform just as much for his part as the first, and in any case according to Luke found recognition and reward, no longer plays a role at the end. Apparently, it is intended to show how the first, and only he, who already possessed so much, is made richer and richer.

The presentation is understandable as soon as one turns to the concluding adage (Mt., v. 29; Lk., v. 26):

To every one who has will more be given, and he will have abundance,
but from him who has not
even what he has will be taken away.

When the contents of this passage are examined, it proves to be a word of wisdom. It expresses an experience of life; we would perhaps say, the poor man never gets on in the world, and the rich man constantly increases his possessions. But in the con-

142

text of Jesus' words, so to speak because of its position, the passage gains a higher significance. It now brings forth a judgment: to those who have produced something it assigns a rich reward and to those who are deemed insufficient the annihilating punishment.

If it is imagined that this pronouncement is bound up with the conjectured original form of the parable, then it is discovered that they harmonize throughout, for the discourse also spoke of sufficient and insufficient, of reward and punishment. But if the concentration on the pivot of the parable is eased and the attention addresses itself equally to both sides, the pleasing as well as the objectionable—if, that is, the proclamation aspires to set up a rounded image of the judgment, then the value of the epigram becomes so much the greater. For now it matches the parable precisely and steps completely into its function; it trains the hearers of the Gospel to reflect upon both the good and the evil departure from earthly life with hope and fear.

From this, the presentation of the punishment becomes comprehensible. Certainly, such a thing was also spoken of in the original parable; indeed, it is an essential part of the conclusion of the case. But it must have been a genuine punishment, of the kind that is described in many of the parables. The bridesmaids are repudiated with the words "I do not know you" (Mt. 25, 12); it is said of the cruel servant, "The Lord delivered him to the jailers" (Mt. 18, 34); and of the other, who abused his power over his fellow servants, "The master of that servant will come . . . and will punish him . . . ?" (Mt. 24, 50). Perhaps closest to what might be conjectured as the original conclusion is the parabolical threat: "And that servant who knew his master's will, but did not make ready or act according to his will, shall receive

143

a severe beating" (Lk. 12, 47). This presentation hits upon the situation precisely, for there is no release from service for a slave; to kill him would be too heavy a penalty; the obvious choice is that he be whipped.

That is a construction, but in the face of such a foil, what actually happened is brought into relief. The maxim has worked its way from the periphery into the story so that its theme has been the determining factor for the story's end. Another conclusion which patterned itself after the maxim was formed out of the given material, and has displaced the original. The advantage was that there could now be seen in the fate of the third servant what the maxim threatened, and in that of the first what it promised.[81]

Here, therefore, arise the discrepancies and discordances which encumber the story. But only those of us who seek the original parable feel this; the proclaimers see it otherwise. They have the judgment in view, and from that view they raise the call of warning and promise before their communities. For them the whole story is an image of the judgment and of its "preliminaries."

God has entrusted the judgment to the "Son of man," and Jesus, the risen and exalted, is the Son of man. If the parable is now viewed as a representational discourse on the judgment, then with a further step it is also interpreted as Christological. This is seen in both versions.

The mighty one, who according to Matthew has the servant thrown out of his house and thrust into the darkness, who makes the one wretched and the other superfluously rich, has long since changed from the man who went on a journey and assigned his slaves to service, to the Lord of the judgment.

Matthew leaves no doubt about this. The intensification already

144

reaches the level to which the image of the world-judgment can attach itself. After the passage of "weeping and gnashing of teeth" he inserts: "When the Son of man comes in his glory, and all the angels with him, then he will sit on his glorious throne. Before him will be gathered all the nations . . ." (25, 31ff.).

Luke achieves the same thing in another way which is complicated, but impressive in its result.

First of all, we must presuppose an independent discourse, lying outside the parable, at the bottom of which there could be a historical event.[82] In the year 4 B.C. the Herodian Archelaos had gone to Rome to have the office of king transferred to him by Caesar. His fellow citizens, who surmised what lay ahead of them, attempted to intervene through a legation. The attempt was fruitless, and as Archelaos returned in the new office he directed a bloodbath against the leading families. This horrible misfortune must have remained in the memory of the people for a long time. Now there is made from this material a pure allegory—probably it is the only one in the entire synoptic tradition. In it the "man of noble birth" who departs in order to receive the kingship represents Jesus, who returns to God and is enthroned in power as the Messiah (cf. Acts 2, 36). In the place of the opposition of his fellow citizens there appears the enmity of Israel towards Him. The return of the king and the annihilation of the rebels is the Parousia and the judgment.

This comprehensive discourse now accompanies the course of the parable tale; it begins before the start of the parable and ends after its conclusion, but it also penetrates it in a few places and changes its form. So the candidate for the throne enters in place of the "man who goes on a journey." The journey not only lasts a long time—this detail is necessary in the parable because only thus is time permitted the servants to trade with the money, —it also leads "into a strange land." When the man returns as king, he makes the servants whose zeal and proficiency have proved themselves in the small task governors over his provinces. In this way, the reward, which Matthew probably preserved from the original, is concretized: "I will set you over much" (vv. 21, 23). The settling of accounts at the end of the parable is changed, too. Here, of course, the allegory does not penetrate but expands the older presentation: the Lord, having returned in His Parousia, creates order in His own house first of all and then turns to His enemies. So the desired complete picture of the judgment arises.

* * *

Luke introduces the version offered by him with the sentence: "He proceeded to tell a parable, because he was near to Jerusalem, and because they [the disciples] supposed that the kingdom of God was to appear immediately" (19, 11). This is an editorial comment; it puts the discourse in a fitting situation and also gives it a certain stress; for now it answers the question when the kingdom of God and with it the messianic exaltation of Jesus will come, and it says *not yet* and *not thus*. It is indeed ordained that the Messiah must go through suffering and death and only thus attain His glory (cf. Lk. 24, 26; Acts 1, 6). The discourse says just that; the Messiah departs, and only when He returns will He wield His power in judgment.

The fully developed discourse which Luke inserts here was probably found thus in his own special matter. But in that case, the version which Matthew offers reached him out of another tradition; in no other way can the differences of the two be comprehended. But because their origin is in one parable of Jesus, there must have first of all been a unified stream of tradition which branched off at a certain point. The adage must have been attached to the parable and reformed its conclusion already before the branching out, for the two versions still agree so far. But in the presentation of the preliminary narrative, too, a certain development of the idea of judgment and along the viewpoint of service and reward must have already begun.[83]

The development has continued after the branching off and both versions exhibit a mature form. Now it must be evaluated.

In Luke, all the servants—there are ten of them, but only three come under careful consideration—receive the same sum; their success, on the other hand, varies. The first adds to his sum tenfold; the second only fivefold. The first is praised and rewarded, but the second also finds the favor of his lord. This presentation makes an assertion: it explains that the justice of the judge will permit even the slightest service to count. In his own way, Matthew makes this entirely clear; he has the lord entrust different sums to his servants in the beginning, and he expressly notes that every man is given "according to his ability" (v. 15). So as the men are different, so also the tasks which are placed upon them differ, and everyone who takes pains according to his strengths shall receive his reward.

The sums confided in Luke's version are trifling; perhaps they are intended to demonstrate the phrase, "You have been faithful in a very little" (v. 17). Matthew, on the other hand, obviously wishes to illustrate how expensive the entrusted property and how great the assigned task are. He names sums which neither the hearers of his Gospel nor he himself could imagine and financially evaluate. It appears that as in the case of the parable of the cruel servant (Mt. 18, 23ff.) he wishes to symbolize quality through quantity. Now he comes upon the phrase of the few and the many, which probably belongs to the original matter of the story, but that does not disturb him, for all that was entrusted and traded with is indeed only a little in comparison to the reward which the great judge awards the loyal. For the level of the story is now left altogether, and the "much" which the servant wins consists of his entering into the joy of his lord. If, as comparable Jewish phrases suggest,[84] the "joy" specifically designates a feast of joy, then, although the discourse remains plastic in its images, it does point to the heavenly banquet of the consummation. With this it becomes clear that the Christological intensification of the parable has also won out within Matthew's version.

* * *

The examination of the two versions of the parable has demanded some effort of the reader. Perhaps it even troubles his straightforward relationship to the Gospel text. The person who does not read "synoptically," of course, scarcely hits upon the question whether the parable of the talents and that of the pounds are not only similar—and in a rather long teaching activity why should the same material not be used in slightly different ways?—but identical. But here the question is asked and answered. So it will be good, after so much analysis, to link together the insights we have gained.

1) It can be seen that behind the canonical Gospels there lies a long process of tradition. A comparison of the texts had made possible conclusions which showed that the stream of tradition had run unified up to a certain point and must then have branched, and it was established with some certainty what form the parable had taken already at the point of branching. So what

was already to be recognized in other parables has been confirmed and verified: tradition does not begin after the completion of the writing of the Gospels, it was already at work long before. It protects the original material and hands it on, but it also concretizes it in the turn of mind, the theology, and the life-interests of the community hearing it. But because both the original discourse and the apostolic proclamation are true, one can join itself to the other. Now the proclamation can influence the original text from the periphery, and thus the differing versions arise.[85]

2) It was also seen here which theme of the apostolic proclamation demonstrates its vigor. It is the insight into the consummation of the messianic way of Jesus and the recognition of His fullness of power to accomplish the judgment of the Last Day as God's vizier; it is, in other words, the Christological theme, which makes it completely necessary for the proclaimers to understand anew the act of judgment of the parable and from it the preceding story, and to explain it accordingly. The complete picture of the judgment is now molded. The loyal servants, their good will, their gain, and their reward find the same attention as the rejected, and the judgment effects salvation as well as damnation.

The version of Luke reaches further and shows how the sentence is passed not only upon the disciples, but also upon the adversaries of the Messiah. The same thing could be seen in the same or reversed series in the transmitted version of the parable of the vinedressers and that of the great banquet, and in the explanation of the parable of the weeds. To recognize one of the main themes of the early Christian proclamation in this manner is not the least fruit of our efforts.

3) The proclamation and its efforts to rely on the words of the

Lord and to present itself in parable must be recognized and evaluated. The original discourse stands out so much the greater. It proves itself of unattainable quality. What Jesus says of God's claim upon the service of man, how He demands the venture-some contribution and declares that it alone corresponds to the will of God: this directive springing out of the original knowl-edge of God's mind is obviously to be found only in Him. No one else has attempted of himself to make something out of such a discourse or to continue the given material on the same plane.

So it is a piece of good fortune, even if perhaps a modest one, that it is possible and permissible for today's exegesis to uncover the piled-up layers and to lay bare what is original in the trans-mitted texts. It is asked why we today should be able to discover and understand what was apparently inaccessible to the exertions of older times. To this it may perhaps be answered that the risk which the theologian approaching the text historically and every-one who listens to him take upon themselves is counterbalanced. In some places there is imparted a knowledge of Jesus and an impression of the depth and clarity of His knowledge of God which may not be compared with more facilely won knowledge in its ability to touch and even shake man's spirit.

4.

After this extended warning to seriousness, the group may be concluded with a double parable which belongs here thematically but which is otherwise modified:

MT. 13, 44–46:
   44 The kingdom of heaven is like treasure hidden in a field, which a man found and covered up; then in his joy he goes and sells all that he has and buys that field.

45 Again, the kingdom of heaven is like a merchant in search of fine pearls,

46 who, on finding one pearl of great value, went and sold all that he had and bought it.

There is the customary introduction which states that one can learn something about the kingdom of God through the following story. It does not compare the kingdom to a treasure any more than it compares it to a salesman in the second verse, but the proceeding which is narrated shows how the parable is related to the kingdom of God. What and how that is must be gathered from the story.

Probably the two parables stand in a contrast similar to that of the building of the tower and of the war: the first treats of a poor, the second of a rich man; what is here made into a parable is found everywhere, among rich or poor. The little farmer, most likely a day laborer, was perhaps at his plough as he uncovered a treasure. That may have happened as is told in a rabbinical story: "Abba Judan went to plough on the other half of the field. As he ploughed, the earth before him opened and his cow stumbled and broke an ankle. He alighted to draw her out. Then God opened his eyes and he found a treasure. He said: 'It is for my own good that the leg of my cow is broken.' "[86] Thus he finds a treasure which someone had buried there a long time before—burying was the most secure protection from robbers—and first of all hides it again.[87] Then he converts all his possessions to money and buys the field. The proceeding perhaps seems somewhat curious in today's legal relationship, but according to Jewish law a field is sold "along with the trash and all that is found therein."[88] The formation of the parable is obvious. The contrast

151

between the apparent folly and the actual wisdom is stimulating. A little worker on the land who pawns his meager possessions, his cattle, and even his house, and who hands over everything because he insists upon having this one field "at any price," can only be viewed with headshaking. But he does it "out of sheer joy." There is a rabbinical parable which uses the same material in similar connection: "It is like a man whose inherited portion was a place full of rubbish. He was indolent and sold it for a pittance. But the buyer went there and dug diligently therein and found a treasure. From it he built a great palace. When the man who had sold it saw this he grew angry and said: 'Woe to me, what a loss have I suffered!' "[89]

The second story states the same thing. The salesman has discovered a precious pearl in a strange land, perhaps at the pearl fisheries, and so he gives over everything that he has brought with him on his pack animals or in his ship for barter and acquires this single pearl. This time it is not said "for sheer joy," but it is understood that the preciousness of the pearl has bewitched him.

In face of the explanations which can be heard for this double parable, it is a good idea to seek the salient point in both stories. It lies solely in that a man, having discovered a good, gives the whole price of which he is capable. To call to mind, for example, the directions given the rich young man, that he should give his possessions to the poor, would do an injustice to the parable. It asserts something greater; it speaks of the kingdom of God and of the prospect of being permitted to live in it when it has come. It says that a man who grasps what God has prepared there for him gives everything for it without hesitation and without lingering, and—and this must appear foolish to those who do not understand—he does it "out of sheer joy."[90]

If the double parable is placed alongside the entire group of parables discussed in the last two chapters, and, of course, in their original form, then a new tone will be perceptible in it. The coming event, and what it brings with it, not only disturbs the indolent calm and lazy peace and shakes men into that watchfulness which is proper for the gravity of the situation, but it also has an attractive power for him who has accepted the message. To see the dominion of God and to take part in the perfected creation within one's own being, means such a piece of good fortune that the fear of God, the seriousness of the decision, and the most extreme effort made for the sake of deliverance is moved and fulfilled and irradiated by a nameless joy.

With some basis it may be conjectured that this parable, like those of the green fig tree, of the growing seed, and of the wedding feast, belongs to the phase of the early Galilean public life. When later on the conflict with Israel determines the themes and, in face of the closedness of the authorities, the decision of the individuals must be battled for, then conceivably the softer theme of enticement subsides. But when the "little flock" which carries on the old promises which were given Israel has experienced the consummation of the messianic work of Jesus, then the theme of joy grows powerful again. A disciple to whom the coming event has come to mean the Second Coming of the Lord who has returned to God, is able to anticipate the raptures of salvation more deeply than any God-fearer of the old time. So it is understandable that without detriment to seriousness, salutary fear, constant vigilance, or humble expectation of the judgment, a man who has begun to grasp the Gospel exists in a joy which is to be compared with no joy in this world.

* * *

From this point, there could once again arise the deeper comprehension of the inflections and explanations of the parables which was to be observed in many examples in just the past two chapters. These were visible in two different procedures. First, the original prophetic warning intended for Israel was directed at the disciples with full force. No Pharisaical conviction of their own justice could arise; no "community of the just" was spared the threat of judgment: it was expressly said that the separation would go through their midst. One need only remember the parable of the banquet in Matthew's version: in order to express this thought, it had drawn upon the parable-fragment of the wedding garment. Alongside it stands the other procedure, which we have in mind here: the parables, through allegorical interpretation, are made into a presentation of the completed salvation. One remembers the parable of the watchful servants (Lk. 12, 35). There, through the explanation of the figure of the master of the house and his slaves waiting in watchful vigilance, through the bringing in of the passage of the banquet by which the Lord showed his love by serving at table, a picture full of glory and bliss arose. The parable of the bridesmaids was similar: as soon as the Lord appearing in the Parousia was discovered in the bridegroom, the rejection of the foolish is no longer the only thing that the parable is intended to portray; in the view of the faithful, the presentation of the banquet of joy belongs to those fortunate ones who had awaited the arrival of the bridegroom in watchful prudence.

154

Such observations can preserve us from feeling that the re-formation of the original sayings of the Lord is arbitrary on the part of the transmitters, as if they had not proceeded carefully from the entrusted materials. The proceeding must be understood differently. It was the riches of the faith which made it almost impossible to perceive the original words with a historical sense. They were not in a position to take their focus from what had become vital truths for them: the *Kyrios* Jesus stands ready for the Parousia and judgment. In the presentiment of that joy they have come to the decision of their lives. What must appear as folly to fools has become for them the highest wisdom.

Notes

[1] G. Dalman, in *Arbeit und Sitte* II, p. 16, reports that an Arab gave him the following explanation for the expression *"karkabas,"* or "arid land": "Something sown upon it comes up quickly and is quickly withered."

[2] *Ibid.*, II, p. 308.

[3] *Ibid.*, III, pp. 163–165.

[4] R. Bultmann, *Synoptische Tradition*, p. 216: "In the case of many parables the original meaning has become unrecognizable in the course of tradition"; among these he numbers the "Parable of the Sower." E. Linnemann, *Gleichnisse Jesu*, p. 175: "I cannot help but look upon the attempts of various exegetes to ascertain even yet the original meaning of the parable as frustrated, for they will be unjust to the historical situation or to the parable or even to both."

[5] The testimony of the early situation, as is seen above all in the concluding statement of verses 33–34[a], certainly belonged to the material Mark had at hand; he himself transformed it by means of certain additions for a late situation, really that of the post-pentecostal community.

[6] Perhaps the parable of the pleading friend (Lk. 11, 5ff.) and of the lazy judge (Lk. 18, 1ff.) were originally joined as a double parable. The key to both is found at the end of the second piece (18, 6–8). It is likewise related to the parables of the shepherd and of the housewife (Lk. 15, 3–10). It remains to be shown that the original key stands in verse 10; verse 7 is formed subsequently from it.

[7] The interpretation has preserved this stress of the text. It speaks not of the sower, but of the seed. "The seed is the word" (4, 14).

[8] The understanding of a parable is not disclosed only through an introductory or concluding key, but also through the application of certain figures emphasized by tradition.

[9] A rabbinical passage: "I had in my garden a mustard shrub on which I climbed as someone is accustomed to climb into the top of a fig tree" (cf. Klostermann on this piece).

[10] Duration of time must not be brought into the interpretation of the parable; cf. J. Gnilka, *Verstockung*, p. 195: "After the period of small beginnings—burdened by failures—of the dominion of God there followed at the end [!] indeed a richer harvest yield."

[11] The term "Sayings of Jesus" refers to a second document of tradition, paralleling the Gospel of Mark, which is not extant but is to some extent recognizable in those sections in which Matthew and Luke agree against or without Mark. The source is designated by the letter "Q."

[12] The stories of the treasure and of the pearl form a genuine double parable (Mt. 13, 44–46). But when the stories of the sowing and that of the weeds, presumably under the influence of the perspective of the accompanying explanations, are grouped together, as has happened in Matthew 13, we have a compilation of two independent parables.

[13] O. Kuss, in "Zum Sinngehalt des Doppelgleichnissess vom Senfkorn und Sauerteig," *Auslegung und Verkuendigung* I, 1963, pp. 78ff., and pp. 85ff., rightly attacks the idea that for the benefit of as crass a contrast as possible the moment of growth in the one and the power of penetration in the other parable are slighted. Of course, that still does not mean that the kingdom of God grows and has a development as such. For a discussion see E. Lohse, "Die Gottesherrschaft in der Gleichnissen Jesu," *Ev. Theol.*, 1958, pp. 145ff., esp. pp. 151–154.

[14] Acts 17, 11: "They received the word with all eagerness." 1 Thes. 1, 6: "You received the word . . . with joy inspired by the Holy Spirit." Jas. 1, 21: "Receive with meekness the implanted word, which is able to save your souls." 1 Pt. 2, 8: "They stumble because they disobey the word." Mk. 1, 45: "He proclaimed and spread the word." 2, 2: "He was preaching the word to them." 8, 32: "He spoke the word openly to them."

[15] V. Taylor, in *The Gospel According to St. Mark,* p. 258, says: "It would be wrong . . . to assume that the interpretation has completely lost touch with the teaching of Jesus. We are not in the presence of pure allegory. The person of the sower is not identified, and no attempt is made, as in later times, to find a hidden significance in the term 'thirtyfold.' . . . In short, the explanation is a partial adaptation of the teaching of Jesus to later conditions."

The parable and the explanations must be seen in contrasting images. Then the change of perspective can be seen, but also at the same time the uniform thematic. For the understanding of that means we are not concerned with the "Undaunted Sower" (J. Jeremias, *Gleichnisse,* p. 130), but with the sowing and its success.

[16] Jeremias, p. 13f.: "The Hebraic word *mashal* designates in the usage of post-biblical Judaism, without resorting to a formal classification, verbal imagery of all kinds: parable, comparison, allegory, fable, adage, apocalyptic revelation, paradox, pseudonym, symbol, invented form, example, model. . . ." See also p. 10, n. 1.

[17] Cf. R. Schnackenburg, *God's Rule and Kingdom.*

[18] In this layer of tradition the report of the demand of the Baptist (Mt. 11, 2ff.[Q]) is clearly related to his beginning sermon.

[19] F. Hauck on this piece: "The parable is to be considered in our place at any case as an insertion since the conclusion ('. . . when you see these things come about') is taken over by verses 24–27." J. Schmid on this piece: "It is clear that the parable of the fig tree can not itself allude to the Parousia, but to the time immediately preceding . . . The parable [does not stand] in its original position here. But the parable also does not form a historical unity with verses 30–32. . . ."

[20] F. Mussner, *Biblische Zeitschrift*, 1962, p. 110: "A striking blindness speaks out of the question of the Pharisees; otherwise they would not, in this situation of salvation history, ask the unusual question of 'when' the kingdom of God will come! They do not recognize that the kingdom of God . . . is already at their disposal through and in Jesus, that it is manifested already at least before their eyes. . . . Jesus therefore answers the question of the Pharisees with a paradox whose meaning is open only to him who in faith is able to join together the kingdom of God and the entrance of the Messiah Jesus."

[21] Cf. W. Bousset, *Die Religion des Judentums* (1926), pp. 222ff.

[22] It could be called the passage of the snatched-away bridegroom. But as Jesus according to the synoptic tradition has probably not presented the Messiah in the figure of the bridegroom any more than the Jewish teachers did, this is not an independent adage, but an addition of the proclaimers. The theme of the passion intervenes in the original text in other places also. In Mt. 12, 40 the sign of Jonas is interpreted. In Mt. 17, 12 the passage on the ill-usage of the Baptist is supplemented by a reference to the passion. In Mk. 10, 45 the adage of the serving Son of man is elucidated by an allusion to the atoning surrender of life. Taylor's interpretation of *Mark*, pp. 210f., is interesting; he considers verses 18–20 a closed unity: "General considerations favor the opinion that γυμφιός is a Messianic expression. Is it likely that Jesus, to whom the Old Testament background . . . was familiar, would use the metaphor of the marriage feast, and apply to Himself the name 'bridegroom,' in a purely general sense? . . . Of course, in 19[a] Jesus does not put forth a public claim to be the Messiah. . . . The implication of the saying is that the Kingdom is already present, that He is its rightful Lord, and that it is incompatible with a situation so joyous that His groomsmen should mourn" (p. 212). "Finally, the poetic structure of 19f. renders the hypothesis of reaction precarious. 19[a] and [b] provide a good example of Semitic parallelism, and there is also a contrast between 19[a] and 20[a] and 19[b] and 20[b]."

[23] H. Schmidt, *Volkserzaehlungen* I, p. 32, as cited in Dalman II, p. 308.

[24] Dalman II, p. 248.

[25] W. Michaelis, *Gleichnisse Jesu*, p. 48: "It presents a warning against feeling with false ardor that one is called to safeguard the purity of the people of God through exclusion or aloofness towards unsuitable elements." Jeremias, p. 189: "It was not only according to the judgment of the Pharisees that there were some among His [Jesus'] disciples who would not stand the test before God. Why did He tolerate this? Why did He not demand that the pure community be sorted out of Israel? Again the scandal at Jesus' attitude becomes an occasion for a double parable. In the two parables of the weeds . . . and of the dragnet . . . Jesus has given the answer."

[26] Bultmann, p. 184: "I designate as genuine parables first of all such forms which are distinguished from a comparison or metaphor only by the minuteness of detail with which the image is formed, and of course a parable can sometimes be developed from a metaphor, sometimes out of a comparison."

[27] Cf. Lv. 11, 9–10: "These you may eat, of all that are in the waters. Everything in the waters that has fins and scales, whether in the seas or in the rivers, you may eat. But anything in the seas or in the rivers that has not fins and scales, of the swarming creatures in the waters and of the living creatures that are in the water, is an abomination to you."

[28] Klosterman on this piece says: "The parable of the dragnet stands close to that of the weeds among the wheat. As the mission is compared to the seed in the first, so it is compared to the fish in the second. The fact that in the first the reader must await the end of a long growth, in the second a short drawing in of fish, is a difference based upon the nature of the image. . . ." Michaelis, p. 69: "While in the parable of the weeds among the wheat a present and a future event are distinguished and only the future event parallels the Last Judgment, even this differentiation is here completely lacking. If what we have here is a view of the Last Judgment, then the catching of the fish already must be thought an introductory part of that event at the end of time. Of course, Jesus' first disciples were fishers of men. Nevertheless, the efficacy of the disciples cannot be meant by the catching of fish. In that case, the sorting out of the fish, an image of the separation at the judgment, would have to be understood as their task. . . ."

[29] This viewpoint can be found in Jeremias, pp. 77, 191.

[30] Not, for example, turned around. For the opposite opinion see Jeremias, p. 72: "The same is also then true for the explanation of the parable of the fish net (Mt. 13, 49f.), which presents merely an abbreviated rendering of 13, 40b–43. . . . We have before us then in Mt. 13, 36–43 and 49–50 two [!] allegorizing explanations of parables from the pen of Matthew."

[31] Klostermann on this piece first of all quotes Wellhausen: "Jesus as Messiah is the viceroy of God, conducts the judgment of the world, has the angels at His disposal," but then narrows this in the usual manner: Matthew makes a distinction between the "kingdom" of the Messiah at hand, in which unworthy members will be found until the judgment itself (in other words the community of the Church) and the future kingdom of the Father. The text gives no basis for such a narrowing. On the other side, cf. Michaelis, p. 51: "The field is explained as the world, that is, men in general, not for example as Israel, and also not as the community of Jesus, which is rather portrayed on one hand by the servants as the disciples of Jesus, and on the other hand by the good wheat."

[32] Here in addition to the already mentioned explanation of the seed as the word and instruction of God (4 Ezra 9, 31), there is another, which is also found in 4 Ezra (8, 41): "For just as the husbandman sows much seed upon the ground . . . and yet not all which were sown shall be saved in due season, . . . so also those that are sown in the world shall not all be saved." Cf. The Psalms of Solomon 14, 3. 4: "The trees of life are his pious ones. Their planting is rooted forever."

[33] These and other conceptions and word-formations betray the disparity between the explanation and the speaking style of Jesus. The word *"kosmos"* for all the inhabited earth does not correspond to the older Hebraic manner of speaking (cf. Dalman, *Die Worte Jesu* I, pp. 132, 145). The expression "sons of evil" is, of course, Semitic, but "the evil one" does not seem to be verifiable as a designation for satan (Foerster and von Rad, *sub* "diabolos," Gerhard Kittel, *Theologishes Woerterbuch zum Neuen Testament* II, pp. 70ff.). Similarly, the expression "sons of the kingdom" is not Jewish, for "kingdom," when not made more specific, refers to the worldly "government" (Dalman, *Worte* I, p. 78).

[34] Dalman, *Arbeit* IV, pp. 327f.: "That fig trees then as today often stood in the vineyard follows from the frequent mention of the vine alongside the fig tree. . . . Now mixed seed is forbidden in a vineyard (Dt. 22, 9). . . . But it is nowhere said that a fig tree or an olive tree may not be planted in the vineyard; . . . it is even mentioned that a vine can be grown on a part of a fig tree or a sycamore. . . ."

[35] Dalman, *Arbeit* IV, pp. 179f.

[36] P. Billerbeck, *Kommentar zum Neuen Testament* II, pp. 197f.

[37] One should not read more into the passage; the application suggested in Jeremias, p. 140, seems artificial.

[38] On the laying out of the vineyard, cf. Dalman, *Arbeit* IV, pp. 317ff.

[39] C. H. Dodd, *The Parables of the Kingdom,* p. 124: "For Juelicher and his followers this is an allegory constructed by the early Church with the death of Jesus in retrospect. I cannot agree. As we shall see, there is

reason to think that it has suffered a certain amount of expansion, but the story in its main lines is natural and realistic in every way. . . . The story has the more verisimilitude if we remember the conditions of the country at the time. Palestine, and Galilee in particular, was a disaffected region. Since the revolt of Judas the Gaulonite in A.D. 6 the country had never been altogether pacified. The unrest had in part economic causes. If now we recall that large estates were often held by foreigners, we may well suppose that agrarian discontent went hand in hand with nationalist feeling, as it did in pre-war Ireland. We can then see that all the conditions were present under which refusal of rent might be the prelude to murder and the forcible seizure of land by the peasantry. The parable, in fact, so far from being an artificially constructed allegory, may be taken as evidence of the kind of thing that went on in Galilee during the half century preceding the general revolt of A.D. 6." For the contrary view, cf. W. G. Kuemmel, *Verheissung und Erfuellung,* pp. 75f.

[40] Verification in Jeremias, 63 A_1.

[41] Verification in Jeremias, *Jerusalem zur Zeit Jesu* II B, p. 200.

[42] Billerbeck III, 20, after listing a series of verifications, states: "In these rabbinical passages the Messiah is called the 'Son' of God only where a messianically interpreted passage of the Old Testament expressly offers occasion for it. As far as we can see, 'Son' of God is not found in the rabbinical literature as an autonomous designation for the Messiah, independent of a scriptural passage. This is astonishing, for in ancient times . . . 'my Son' was definitely used in the mouth of God as an independent designation for the Messiah. One will not err if one assumes that the rabbinical scholars have intentionally avoided the expression 'Son' of God as such because it has in the meanwhile become a current designation for the Messiah among the Christians." For a discussion, cf. O. Cullmann, *Die Christologie des Neuen Testaments,* pp. 279ff.

If it may be assumed that in the surroundings of Jesus the Messiah could be designated as "Son," then the opposite is also true, that the title of Son in the synoptic reports (cf. Mk. 1, 11; 9, 7) is intended primarily to name the Messiah and express the nearness to God in which the Messiah as the "beloved" of God stands. This title deepens with the continuing insight into the mystery of Jesus and leads to assertions like Phil. 2, 5ff.; Col. 1, 15ff.; Jn. 1, 1ff., but also even to Gal. 4, 4ff. At the point of the shift into this deeper meaning there stands the passage transmitted in the sayings of Jesus found in Mt. 11, 27 = Lk. 10, 22. But knowledge of Jesus never detaches itself completely from the messianic terminology, which remains preserved throughout all testimony.

[43] In the collection of sayings of the so-called Gospel of Thomas there stands as verse 66:

"He said:
A good man had a vineyard;
he gave it to farmers
that they might till it
and he might receive its fruit from them.
He sent his slave
so that the farmers might give him
the fruit of the vineyard.
They overpowered the slave [and] beat him.
They all but killed him.
The slave came [and] told it to his master.
His master said,
Perhaps he did not know them.
He sent another slave; the farmers beat the
other.
Then the master sent his son.
He said, Perhaps they will reverence my son.
Since those farmers knew
that he was the heir of the vineyard,
they seized him [and] killed him.
He who has ears, let him hear!"

[44] Billerbeck I, pp. 875f.

[45] H.-J. Kraus, *Psalmen*, p. 807: "The wonderful turning point of life is caught in a clear image. He who is thrown into the sphere of death resembles a stone which the builders threw away as useless. But this stone has been raised to the honor of the cornerstone. . . . Someone despised has been brought to honor. One ordained to death is allowed to live."

[46] Billerbeck I, p. 880.

[47] Billerbeck IV, pp. 1145f.; in the Gospels: Lk. 14, 15; Mt. 8, 11; Lk. 22, 30; Mk. 14, 25.

[48] The expression "before you" is intended to translate the Aramaic "*min,*" through which the intensification is expressed: "rather than you." For this the context indicates one exclusive sense, as in the phrase of the psalm, "He anointed you 'before' your companions," that is, you, and not your companions. Cf. Jeremias, p. 123.

[49] W. Trilling, "Zur Ueberlieferungsgeschichte des Gleichnisses vom Hochzeitsmahl, Mt. 22, 1–14," in *Biblische Zeitschrift,* 1962, pp. 251ff.

[50] Klostermann on this point: "The already doubtful assumption that those invited later are, in accordance with Oriental customs, offered a wedding garment which they then disdained, would by no means fit here. The reproach . . . is not directed at the fact that the guest has declined [the wedding garment]."

162

[51] The assumption of a fragment stands between the interpretation that this is a finished, originally independent parable (M.-J. Lagrange, T. W. Manson, J. Schmid, T. Jeremias, E. Lohmeyer, W. Michaelis), and the other view that it is only an allegorizing expansion of the parable (for example, A. Juelicher, A. Loisy, R. Bultmann, W. Trilling).

[52] Billerbeck I, p. 878.

[53] *Ibid*. This is not to say that Matthew or his model allegorize in such a fashion. E. Neuhaeusler, *Anspruch und Antwort Gottes,* pp. 217ff.: "Probably we may not interpret the wedding garment any more than the burning lamps . . . of the maidens . . . ; the lacking of the wedding garment should only elucidate the lack of preparedness."

[54] Jeremias, 49 A 2, notes that the Aramaic word "hanephā" means not only "hypocrite" but also "godless," "impious." Correspondingly, Mk. 8, 15 warns of the "leaven of the Pharisees"; "leaven," however, is a metaphor for the evil pagan disposition (cf. Billerbeck I, p. 729 [*sub* c]). This disposition is designated in the parallel passage in Luke (12, 1) as "*hypokrisis.*" There is thus more than a hypocritical manner that is involved; Luke hits the mark when he says, "He will give him a place among the unbelievers."

[55] Hauck says of Lk. 12, 41: "Luke, who interrupts the longer discourses and places value on identifying the persons addressed, forms the transition with a question of Peter which narrows the following parable to the disciples as holders of an office."

[56] Klostermann says of Lk. 12, 36: "While '*gámos*' is not here the real wedding of the Lord, and perhaps really only means 'dinner,' so also the influence of Mt. 25, 1ff. is not probable, especially as it is not even the guests outside who knock afterwards, but rather the lord who desires entrance by knocking."

[57] Cf. the analysis in Dodd, pp. 161–167.

[58] Hauck writes of Lk. 22, 27: "Verse 27 contains a parable passage in 27ᵃ which appears in an expanded form in Luke in the situation of the Last Supper, in Mark (10, 45) at Jesus' sacrifice of His life. In John, the same idea is detailed still further at the washing of the feet."

[59] This interpretation is especially sharply advocated by G. Bornkamm in the second part of the essay "Die Verzoegerung der Parusie" (ed. W. Schmauch, *In Memoriam E. Lohmeyer,* 1951), pp. 119ff.

[60] Cf. the critical presentation of the problem and a development of this thesis in Linnemann, pp. 130ff. and 182ff.

[61] Jeremias, pp. 157ff. Jeremias does not maintain that the usages of today are the same as those of the time of Jesus, but he shows that the course of events described in the parable is possible and therefore meaningful.

[62] Cf. Billerbeck I, pp. 504–517.

[63] Cf. the reports reproduced in Jeremias, pp. 158ff.

[64] Billerbeck I, p. 970.

[65] It is reported of Arabic weddings that the family of the bride often haggles with the bridegroom for a long time about the presents which are to be made to the nearest relatives of the bride. Even this proceeding is part of the ritual, for it is intended to demonstrate the value of the bride. So a factual basis is supplied for the procrastination. The detail, of course, cannot be transferred without ado to the old wedding celebration, but it can be seen that the delay can have a natural basis. Cf. Jeremias, p. 159.

[66] There is a proverb to express that an opportunity passed up does not easily return: "The door that is closed is not quickly opened." Billerbeck I, p. 970.

[67] H. Schleier in Kittel I, pp. 341, l. 34:

". . . Through the placing of the 'Amen' before Jesus' own words the passage is marked as something which is certain and reliable, and in fact certain and valid because at the same time Jesus acknowledges his own words with the 'Amen' and makes them binding for himself."

[68] Hauck, *Luke*, p. 184: "Verse 25 is a fragment of the eschatological parable."

[69] In the original parable the delay of the bridegroom is a detail ordained by the logic of the tale, and therefore in itself of no allegorizing moment. J. Schmid on this piece: "Neither the long absence of the bridegroom nor the falling asleep of the maidens occasioned by it . . . is important for the explanation of the parable. That both these details are unusual, 'improbable,' does not yet prove that they are there only in regard to the religious reality, and must be explained allegorically." Indeed, it can never be asserted of the proclamation that it has seen in the delay a portrayal of the failure of the Parousia to take place.

[70] The difficult translation of Mt. 11, 12 is discussed by Neuhaeusler, pp. 81–84. We agree when he says in note 134: "Mt. 11, 12[b], in the form in which it is transmitted, lets the reader think of the violence and plundering of the *basileia* really only in a negative sense. The tautology resulting from such an explanation can be no serious objection, for it could, as intended by Matthew, wish to emphasize just this seriousness of the situation." He continues: "Nevertheless, difficulties intrinsic to this interpretation remain. It is not possible to classify this verse anywhere in the synoptic proclamation." This difficulty arises as soon as a seriously ironic manner of speaking, which can be seen in other statements of Jesus, is noted.

[71] Logion 95[98] from the Gospel of Thomas could perhaps be placed alongside the double parable: "Jesus said: The Kingdom of the Father

is like a man who wishes to kill a powerful man. He drew a sword in his house, he stuck it into the wall, in order to know whether his hand would carry through; then he slew the powerful man."

[72] Hauck says of this piece: "Both parables wish to express what a difficult undertaking the following of Jesus is. Whoever is ready for it must seriously examine himself to determine whether he has the strength to carry the resolve to the end, and if not, rather foresee that from the very beginning[!]. Thus Jesus, who disdains propaganda with illusory promises, Himself warns of every unconsidered connection on the matter." Similarly, J. Schmid says on this: "Just this union of the double parable with the thoughts of following Jesus, however, appears to create a difficult theological problem; for the inference which should be drawn from it can only be this: He who wishes to undertake the difficult task of following Christ must first of all examine his strength, and if he perceives that he has not grown to this task, then he should from the beginning not venture on it. Only in this way can he avoid a catastrophe. But according to the Gospel there is a twofold way of imitating Jesus, one to which all who perceive the call of Jesus are obligated, and a special one which exists in a personal joining to Him and demands the greatest sacrifice, to which not everyone is grown." The solution of the perceived problem is thus seen in that the parable speaks only of the special imitation of those wandering with Jesus. If one nevertheless proceeds from the recognition that the parable originally speaks of the effort which is to be made in the face of the coming experience, then it becomes clear that the concretizing which tradition has undertaken aims first of all at the fundamental discipleship, and that the special form of life of the most narrow circle is touched upon by the parable only secondarily and in analogy.

[73] The same thing appears in the example in Mt. 19, 30—20, 15. There the succession of epigrams, as the Mark parallel 10, 31 shows, had concluded with the adage: "But many that are first will be last, and the last first." To this Matthew has annexed the parable of the master of the laborers which he had in his special matter and then repeated, "So the last will be first, and the first last."

[74] Kittel, I, pp. 213-215. K. H. Schelkle, *Discipleship and Priesthood.*

[75] Matthew facilitates the understanding in the parallel passage 10, 37: "He who loves father or mother more than me. . . ."

[76] Cf. Hauck, *Luke,* Appendix 12: "The words of Luke show the attitude of Jesus with a certain intensification. This hardly stems from the transfer of the words into the Hellenistic world. At least Paul shows nothing similar. Much more likely, the formulations in Luke descend from the circles of the poor Palestinian Jewish Christians. . . . On the other hand, the sharp condemnation of Luke's words seemingly concurs

with a certain 'anti-property' manner of thinking of the narrator himself. The life of poverty of the community in mutual brotherliness for him is the obvious realization of an ideal that also corresponded precisely to Hellenistic thought."

[77] There is an instructive rabbinical parallel to this. R. Eleazar: "I wish to tell you a parable. With what can the matter be compared? With a man to whom the king deposited something for safekeeping. Every day he wept and cried: Woe is me, when will I be rid of this burden in peace?" (Billerbeck I, p. 971). Here the parable is told as consolation to a father whose son has died. But in any case it proceeds from the earthly experience that being entrusted with something by a mighty person is a source of anxiety.

[78] Neuhaeusler, p. 104: "To himself the lazy servant seems blameless. In the human sense he was not lazy. His fault was something else. Even the lord himself remained as alien to him as the money in his hands. He feared him in his strangeness. By this Jesus wishes to say that the act of obedience to a God who is in this way alien is intrinsically corrupted. In the face of a hard God, man can only obey legalistically. His obedience, however, does not unfold itself in creative and willing acquiescence in every demonstration of confidence of his Lord."

[79] The judgment of Jesus on the Pharisees is of greater severity. Nevertheless, it is to be pondered that the individual man is not condemned. What Jesus rejects is a conduct towards God that results from the Pharisaical teaching. To pass over the subjective frame of the individual and to sketch the false attitude is a legitimate means of prophetic warning.

[80] Dodd, pp. 151f.: "Who is the servant of God, who is condemned for an overcaution amounting to breach of trust? I would suggest, that he is the type of pious Jew who comes in for so much criticism in the Gospels. He seeks personal security in a meticulous observance of the Law. . . . The parable, I suggest, was intended to lead such persons to see their conduct in its true light. They are not giving God His own; they are defrauding Him. . . . To abandon the scrupulous discipline of Pharisaism would be a risk, no doubt. It was precisely the risk that the early Christians took, and they took it under the inspiration of their Master. It is the kind of risk, this parable suggests, that all investment of capital involves; but for the risk of investment, the capital remains fruitless. We have here, it seems, a pointed application of the parable which arises directly out of the historical situation."

[81] It is thus not said that the conclusion of the parable has annexed the adage—cf. Jeremias, p. 54; Schmid on Mt. 25, 29—but vice versa: the joined adage has changed the parable's conclusion.

[82] This is not to assert that such an event actually was the basis, and

166

above all not that this is an independent parable of Jesus. For another view, cf. Jeremias, pp. 50f.

[83] Cf. the similar presentation of the history of tradition in Dodd, pp. 152f.

[84] Billerbeck I, p. 972: "The expressions mean, nonetheless, not only joy, but also a feast of joy, in particular a wedding. 'Chara' can also be intended here in the sense of a banquet of joy." For a more precise treatment, cf. Dalman, *Worte* I, p. 96.

[85] The recognition that neither the one nor the other version enjoys precedence of age was important. One ought not dispute this. The attempt, for example, to explain the presentation of Luke as closer to the original does not at all free us from the question of what then has happened in Matthew. Even if changes in the original wording are acknowledged, a more basic analysis adds no further problems. Those which nevertheless are outstanding will have to be dealt with by a theological insight.

[86] Billerbeck I, p. 674.

[87] As the Semitic languages have no compound verbs, the "again" must be completed. For a translation into German, cf. Jeremias, pp. 167f.

[88] Verification in Billerbeck I, p. 674.

[89] *Ibid.*

[90] Jeremias, p. 169: "It is not the sacrifice of the two men . . . which is the deciding factor, but the occasion for their sacrifice: the being overcome by the size of their discovery. So is it with the royal dominion of God. The joyful message overwhelms, gives great joy, directs the entire life towards the perfection of the community of God, effects the most passionate surrender."

Biblical References

EXODUS

Chapter	Verse	Page
19	17	119

DEUTERONOMY

Chapter	Verse	Page
20	19	69
33	2	119
	3	119
	4	119

JOSHUA

Chapter	Verse	Page
2	21f.	122

2 SAMUEL

Chapter	Verse	Page
7	14	78

JOB

Chapter	Verse	Page
21	7–18	54

PSALMS

Chapter	Verse	Page
2	7	78
10	1–6	54f.
14		109
73	2–4	55
	10–12	55
80		69
111	10	102

ISAIAH

Chapter	Verse	Page
1	21	71
2	2–6	88
5	1–2	73
	4	70
	5–7	70
45	6	88
49	12	88
55	10–11	22
57	3	71
59	19	88

JEREMIAH

Chapter	Verse	Page
2	2	122
3	3	71
	18	88
12	7	122
23	29	22

EZEKIEL

Chapter	Verse	Page
16	8	122
17	5	69
19	10	69

DANIEL

Chapter	Verse	Page
12	3	65

HOSEA

Chapter	Verse	Page
2	2	71

JOEL

Chapter	Verse	Page
4	13	53

MALACHI

Chapter	Verse	Page
1	10ff.	88

DIDACHE

Chapter	Verse	Page
10	6	116

4 ESDRAS

Chapter	Verse	Page
9	30–33	21

MATTHEW

Chapter	Verse	Page
3	7–12	41
	9	131
	10	41
	12	41, 53
4	1–10	28
	19ff.	130
6	19–21	31
	24–33	31
7	1	60

	21ff.	101	18	23ff.	147
	23	122		34	143
	24ff.	32, 127	20	16	137
8	11	115, 131	21—25		89
	11f.	82, 89	21	1	96
10	22	131	21, 1—24, 3		89
	34–36	123		10–17	89
11	12	125		18f.	89
	18–19	47		18–32	89
13	16f.	43		20–22	89
	24ff.	96		23	96
	24–30	52		23–27	89
	26	53		31	91
	27	53		33	73
	31	61		33–41	72
	33	26		33–46	89
	34–35	34		34	97
	36–43	62		35	97
	37–39	62		36	97
	40	62		37	74
	40–43	62ff.		39	74
	41	62		41	74, 97
	42	62		42f.	96
	43	66		42–46	96
	44	150		43	101
	44–46	150f.	22	1–14	89
	45–46	151		2–3	84
	47f.	54		2–10	84ff.
	47ff.	54		3	94, 97
	47–50	58		4	94
	49	59	22	4–9	85
	49a	62		5	94
	49b	62		6	94
	49f.	63		7	95
	50	62		8	87
	51f.	61		9–10	86, 92
15	8–9	139		11–14	98f.
17	20	23		13	137

Ch.	Verse	Page	Ch.	Verse	Page
	14	102, 137		28	136, 138, 141
	15–22	89		29	136, 142
	23–33	89		30	135f.
	34–40	89		31–32	65
	41–46	89		31ff.	145
23	1–36	89		32	60
	4	140	28	19f.	101
	8–10	111	MARK		
	13	139	1	14–15	21
	23ff.	139		17	59
23, 27—24, 3		89		17f.	128
23, 27—25, 46		65		22	21f., 40
24		98		23–28	21
	44	123		27	40
	45–47	114		27–28	21
	45–51	108f.		32–34	21
	50	143		38	24
25	1	132		38–40	21
	1ff.	113		40–43	21
	1–13	117f.		45	21
	12	143	2	2	21
	13	124, 137		7	22
	14	135		8–12	21
	14–15	132		13	21
	14–30	132ff.		13–17	58
	15	135, 147		14	128
	16–18	135		16	22
	16–22	133		18–19	46
	19	135		18–22	45ff.
	20–23	135		18ff.	96
	21	146		19	114
	23	146		20	48, 50
	23–29	134		21–22	47, 49
	24–25	136		23	48
	24–27	138		24	22
	25	138	3	1–6	21
	26	138		2	22
	26–27	136		4	140

	7–12	21	
	20–30	22	
	22	22, 67	
	22–27	21	
	31–35	21	
4	1–2	18	
	2	29	9
	3	16	10
	3–8	15	
	3–9	15ff.	
	4	20	12
	5–6	16	
	7	17	
	8	17	
	8–9	16	13
	10	17	
	10–13	28	
	11	36	
	13	17	
	14	29, 31	
	14–20	17, 28	
	14ff.	96	16
	15	29	
	16–17	30	3
	18–19	30	
	20	31	4
	21–23	33	
	21–25	28, 33	5
	24–25	33	
	25	137	7
	26–29	23	
	30–32	24	
	33–34	33, 34	
	34b	34	
6	7	128	
	12f.	128	8
7	1	67	
8	12	71	9

32	56	
32f.	35	
33b	57	
34–38	128	
35	130	
38	71	
33ff.	35	
17ff.	129	
35ff.	35, 56	
42–44	111	
1	73	
1–9	72	
5	73	
8	74	
24–27	42	
28f.	42	
33	107	
33–37	106	
34	61, 107	
35a	107	
36	107	
17f.	51	
LUKE		
17	41	
17–18	41	
1–12	28	
18b	21	
10	59	
11	128	
7–10	114	
16	40	
31–34	71	
33–35	72	
36	67, 91	
36ff.	67, 141	
9	35	
15	31	
1–2	128	

	6	128		25–27	123
	23–26	128		28	89
	24	130		28–30	82
	51ff.	56	14	1	67
	51–56	55		1–24	91
	59	128		7–11	92
	62	127		13	93
10	1	128		15	91
	9	128		16–17	84
	23f.	43		16–24	84
	26	46		18–23	85
11	20	44		21	92, 95
	37	67		23	92
	42	139		23–24	86
12	15–21	31		24	87
	32	103		25–27	127, 129
	33	130		28–32	126
	35	154		33	127
	35ff.	111	15	1	141
	35–38	112		10	68
	36	108		11	91
	36[a]	107	16	16	125
	37[a]	107	17	7	115
	37[b]	113f.		20f.	44
	38	107	18	9	91, 93
	39f.	105, 111		19	93
	41	111		28ff.	129
	41–46	108	19	1	91
	47	111, 144		7	141
	51–53	129		11	146
13	1–5	56		11–13	132
	3	70		11–27	132ff.
	6–9	68		12	135
	15	140		12–27	135
	16	140		13	135
	19–21	25		14	135
	20f.	26		14–18	133
	24	125		15	135

	16–19	135		52	65
	17	147	16	22	116
	19–26	134		**2 CORINTHIANS**	
	20–21	136	4	16–18	51
	20–23	138	11	2	50, 122
	22–23	136		**GALATIANS**	
	24	141	1	4	51
	24f.	136, 138		**EPHESIANS**	
	26	136, 142	5	25	50
	27	135f.		25–27	122
20	9	73		**1 THESSALONIANS**	
	9–16	72	4	15–17	104
	12	73		16–17	65
	13	74	5	2	104, 106, 124
	15	74		4	106, 124
21	31	43		6	104
22	18	115		**2 THESSALONIANS**	
	27	115	1	7–10	65
	30	115f., 124	2	1ff.	104
24	26	146		**1 TIMOTHY**	
	JOHN		3	15	110
3	29	50, 123		**HEBREWS**	
4	1	67	3	6	110
13	1ff.	115	13	11–13	82
	ACTS			**1 PETER**	
1	6	146	2	4	83
	6f.	57		6	83
2	30–33	65	4	17	110
	36	145	5	2ff.	110
3	21	65		**2 PETER**	
4	10–12	83	3	10	106
10	38	21		**REVELATION**	
	ROMANS		3	3	106
8	18	51		20	116
9—11		90	16	15	106, 124
11	17	69	19	7	123
13	11ff.	104	21	1	123
	1 CORINTHIANS			9	123
15	24–28	63	22	17	116, 123

CARMELITE MONASTERY
Beckley Hill
Barre, Vt., 05641

DATE BORROWED